God's

Magnum

Opus

The Value of a Woman

VICTORIA BOYSON

God's
Magnum
Opus

Victoria Boyson Ministries
www.VictoriaBoyson.com
Victoria@Boyson.org

For My Daughters,
Cassandra and CailieEllen

CONTENTS

FOREWORD

Now Is the Time for Godly Women to Arise!

Now is the time for godly women as role models to emerge on the scene of church history and extend their influence into all of the seven cultural mountains! Just like Barak and Deborah, we need men and women to work together. As a coach and a champion for women in leadership and ministry, I want to see a company of Deborahs arise in this hour across the spectrum of society.

"That the leaders led in Israel, that the people volunteered, Bless the Lord!" Judges 5:2 NASV

Yes, it is a rather intense story found right in the middle of the pages of Bible concerning Deborah the Deliverer (read Judges 4 & 5). But as a male spiritual leader, I have something to say to you mighty women of God! We cannot afford for you to be fearful "little women" in your own eyes. It is time for you to Emerge! We need you!

Instead, you must come forth with internal security like Deborah of old and pick up your warrior's mantle for such a time as this. Today, across the globe and right in our own back yards, there are enemies on the rampage tearing apart society at every corner. My late wife, Michal Ann Goll, and I founded the Women on the Frontlines conference movement. In her inaugural book, Women on the Frontlines – A Call to Courage, she issued a clarion call that still needs answered today.

We live in an age that is sorely lacking in heroes.

Think about it. Who can we look at today and regard as a hero? Certainly there are some, but they sure are hard to find! Isaiah the prophet said that when a people comes under judgment, God takes away wise leadership from the land—the hero, warrior, judge, prophet, elders and others (see Isaiah 3:1-4 NIV). During a time of restoration the Lord restores the Land. We are now entering a time of restoration, and the Lord is calling us to be heroes. He is preparing us for a time soon to come when the world will cry out for leaders who are in touch with the heart and the mind of God. (Michal Ann Goll, Women on the Frontlines, (Shippensburg, PA: Destiny Image Publishers, Inc., 1999) 145.)

So with the voice of my late wife, Michal Ann Goll, still echoing in the shadows, a new breed of women leaders like Victoria Boyson are now emerging. There is a modern day women's movement that cannot be stopped appearing on the global scene today. Together we echo loud and clear, "It's time to arise and carry Deborah's heart and anointing!" Yes, it must be a heart of purity mixed with the unshakeable quality of courage.

In the midst of this new women's movement, we must hold close to our heart the teachings of Zechariah 7:9-10 (AMP) which says, "Thus has the Lord of hosts said, Dispense true justice and practice kindness and compassion each to his brother; and do not oppress the orphan, the stranger or the poor; and do not devise evil in your hearts against one another."

Who was Deborah anyway? She was a Prophetess, a Judge, a Wife, a Warrior, and a Worshiper of her God and ultimate King. Deborah brought healing, deliverance and restoration to her land. She changed the justice system and she brought trade and commerce back to her people. She and Barak joined together in the infamous battle against Sisera, and won!

It's time for men and women to join together and provide real leadership and justice like Deborah and Barak! As a male spiritual leader in the global prayer and prophetic movement, I say to you, "Come Forth!" Come on now! Change society. Shift the courts. Bring revival and restoration to the land.

The book you hold in your hand is an excellent treasure to be added to the voices who have gone before. Victoria Boyson is a brave, mature and pure voice from the Lord. I am grateful to the Lord for this excellent book you hold in your hand! I highly commend to you the writings, the ministry and the life of another one of God's Girls in this hour!

Remember, You Were Chosen for Such a Time as This!

Dr. James W. Goll

Encounters Network • Prayer Storm • Compassion Acts

Best Selling Author

Dr. James Goll is a Best Selling Author, Founder of Encounters Network, Prayer Storm and helps carry on the work of Compassion Acts. For information on his online school visit: GETeSchool.com. James continues to live in TN and is a joyful father and grandfather today.

I

Magnum Opus

"Every good and perfect gift is from above, coming down
from the Father of the heavenly lights, who does not
change like shifting shadows" James 1:17 NIV.

The Father's Truth

WHO DO YOU think understands your real value?
Do you feel your family or friends know your true
worth? Do you turn to your spouse or parents to
estimate your value? Are you a fair judge of your own
personal merit?

There is only ONE accurate estimation of your
worth and that is *the Father's*. You cannot count on
any person to give you a true calculation of your
value. Indeed, only your heavenly Father understands
your correct standing, because you are *His* creation.

Your heavenly Father has known you from your
mother's womb. Only He really understands you and
the things that have fought hard to wound your soul
and steal your confidence. He sees you through eyes
uncluttered by human hindrances and social
sentiment.

God sees you as the perfect gift He destined you
to be to the earth. For, "When God created mankind,

he made *them* in the likeness of God. He created *them male and female* and blessed *them*. And he named them 'Mankind' when *they* were created" Genesis 5:1-2 (NIV emphasis mine). He saw you then as He sees you now: a miracle of promise to the earth!

So, if your Father alone knows your true worth, it makes sense that you should look only to Him for your personal evaluation and guidance for your future. If you are to fulfill your destiny in Christ, you must fight to make God the mirror of your competency and ability. All other messages sent to captivate your attention and warp your opinion of yourself must be cast down if you are to develop your voice for Him.

Hibiscus Bush

When my family and I moved from Iowa to Texas, I was so excited to be in a region of the United States where tropical plants would flourish. I purchased and planted several hibiscus bushes and most of them did quite well, but one particular bush was dwarfed in comparison to the others. It refused to grow and its leaves eventually turned yellow and died.

I struggled with the bush for months and babied it with special powders and fertilizers, but to no avail.

Later that year, a polar vortex (cold spell) hit Texas, and along with my failing bush, all the tropical plants I planted were killed. As I pulled up the dead plants to start over, I saw that the troubled bush I had struggled to keep alive had grubs in its roots and was slowly being devoured by them. It had been the nasty grubs all along that had kept it from growing and becoming the beautiful bush it was purposed to be.

I began to realize how we, as humans, have similar troubles—little lies attacking our roots at our foundation. Inaccurate thoughts we have believed about ourselves have been the culprits of our demise and have kept us from growing, maturing and bearing fruit. It is the lies the enemy plants in our minds that keep us from thriving and living in more than just merely a survival mode.

Cassandra's Trial

My oldest daughter, Cassandra, loves God passionately and grew up with such a vibrant openness, loving everyone. When she was only seven years old and just starting to read, I found her alone in her room with her Bible in her lap crying uncontrollably. She couldn't even breath, she cried so hard, and when I asked her why, all she could say was, "So many people are going to hell, Mama."

The overwhelming thought of lost souls seemed to possess her. With almost every friendship she had, she drew them to the Lord. Truth be told, their parents didn't always like it when their children were saved and filled with the Spirit and came home praying in tongues.

One of Cassandra's favorite things to do was to have what she called a revival on Halloween. Blaring Christian music from her CD player for all the neighbors to hear, she would stand outside on our front porch and shout for passersby to come to our house and get saved. As far as she knew, she believed she would, indeed, win the world to Jesus. Even as a child, she had intense purpose and passion—it was beautiful.

Cassandra was only twelve when our dream of putting our children into Christian school was realized. Unfortunately, this dream turned into a nightmare when her teacher taught the kids in her class that women were not allowed to be in ministry or even to pray when men were present. She actually taught the young girls and boys of her class that women were second-class citizens, created that way by God. In every possible way, she indicated that girls were not as good as boys and they absolutely could never be in ministry.

Naturally, I felt compelled to confront the teacher about what she was teaching my daughter and it was then I realized the erroneous teachings were in her very deep. She considered my objections against her to be persecution, and instead of seeing the pain she had caused, she saw herself as a martyr for what she believed.

I realized there was nothing I could say to her that would change the way she believed. Even after hearing our objections against this doctrine, she refused to allow the girls in her class to pray. Quite the contrary, she used the incident to make the point that God only wants men to lead in religious activities and that no woman is the equal of a man.

Through the time Cassandra was in her class, she repeatedly made it clear that women and even young girls were never to be in any type of ministry. The mere thought that this could be true was devastating to Cassandra. You can probably imagine the effects of a teacher saying that to a 12 year old girl who wants only to serve God.

At the end of the school year, Cassandra came to

me and asked, "Mom, why was I even born?" She felt like God did not like her, approve of her or love her.

I tried very hard to convince her that God valued her and loved her. But it seemed that no matter what I said to her, the little lies about women from this teacher were chewing away at the roots of her faith, destroying her joy and purpose in life, even her relationship with God.

The Battle for Destiny

From the time she was seven years old, Cassandra loved God with a great passion and wanted nothing more than to grow up and become a preacher and save souls. Now, just a mere five years later, this beautiful, passionate, flowering "bush" was being eaten alive by the enemy's devastating lies about women and literally stripped her of her life's purpose.

As her Mom, I truly fought hard to prove to her the lies about women were just that, but she was not easily convinced. It did not help that the attack against her was backed by other sources as well. The enemy will always hit you where you are already weak and he compounded the lies in Cassandra's mind as we fought hard to dispel them. It was, indeed, a battle for her destiny, her soul and even her life. Barely giving her a chance to breath, the enemy continued to pour his poison into her life and brought wave after wave of devastation through one misguided, reckless individual after another.

Honestly, it is difficult for me to think back at the attacks the enemy threw at her during this time. It changed her from being a perky, trusting girl, to being extremely guarded and shy. It wasn't just her destiny the enemy was after, he wanted to take her life. By destroying her life's purpose, he could then make life unbearable to live—life purpose is *that important*.

At this point, she decided to fight back, but needed proof to fight with and came to me for answers. Diving into the Word of God, I purposed myself to find anything and everything I could to prove to her, first, that God loved her and fashioned her to be a woman and, second, that her calling to minister was a gift from her heavenly Father who loves her!

The fruit of my study to save Cassandra is the product of this book!

Genesis' Truth

If you want to determine what God really thinks of women, you have to go back to the beginning, back to the moment He presented women to His creation. His purpose was to create something so uniquely treasured for a most beloved friend—Adam. God loved Adam so much that He wanted to truly bless him with the most precious gift He had ever created. It was His love for Adam that compelled Him to make woman His magnum opus—His great masterpiece of creation.

In Genesis 2:18, the LORD God said, "It is *not good* for the man to be alone; I will make him a helper suitable for him." (NIV emphasis mine)

God looked at all creation and said, "This is NOT GOOD!" because it wasn't finished. He had yet to give Adam his greatest gift—woman. In the creation story, paradise was not complete until God created Eve.

After God created the woman, "God saw all that He had made, and it was *very good*," (Genesis 1:31 NIV emphasis mine). God stepped back and took a sigh of great pleasure and saw that what He had desired to create was finally finished and it brought Him great joy.

God paused in the middle of the sixth day and said, "not good." Then He declared it to be "very good" only *after* He created woman.

It was *very good* because God had intended to bless Adam with one of His most creative treasures. Anticipating Adam's delight in her, the Father longed to see His daughter appreciated and loved.

In Hebrew, the meaning of the words God used to refer to the woman in Genesis 2:18, "I will make him a *helper suitable* for him," are very interesting. The word "helper" is *ezer* in Hebrew and is actually translated more accurately to mean "powerful helper." Every other time the word *ezer* is used in Scripture, it is referring to God or the Holy Spirit, Who was sent to be our Helper, Comforter and Guide (John 14:26).

God did not intend to give Adam a gift of lesser value. No, God never gives *cheap gifts*! He gave Adam a companion who could really be of great help to him. She was designed by God with different but equal strengths to assist Adam and he, in turn, helps her. Working perfectly in line with one another, He intended they should help each other. Neither was greater or lesser, just different.

The Hebrew word for "suitable," being *kneged*, means equal. Obviously, this makes a great deal of sense, because woman was to be an adequate help to him. If she were not his equal, she would not be much help at all, but someone he had to constantly pull up to his level. If God had not used the word "suitable," and only referenced ezer it would mean that women were greater than men. But His design was that they would be one flesh. Truly, they could not be one if they were not equal.

Think about it...if you had trouble with your computer, would you ask someone for help who knew nothing about computers? No, of course not. You would consult someone who could actually be a help to you. Does helping others make you less of a person? Is a teacher less than the student just because they help them?

It was God's plan and delight that Adam and Eve would *reign together in unity as equal partners*.

He said in Genesis 1:26, "Let us make human beings in our image, to be like us. *They will reign over* the fish in the sea, the birds in the sky, the livestock, all the wild animals on the earth, and the small animals that scurry along the ground" (NLT).

Not Property

God the Father did not create Eve to become Adam's property, nor did He create any human being to become anyone's property. On the contrary, she was created to be a cherished companion. As Adam stated when he referred to Eve, "The woman whom You gave *to be with me*" (Genesis 3:12 NASB). She was meant to be a companion, not property. A treasure to Adam, Eve was not created to be used, but to be loved and love in return.

God loved Adam so much, He created the greatest, most inspiring work of art He could for him.

Truly, the Father loves humanity so much that it's difficult to even find words to describe the love He feels for mankind. If we truly understood the love He has for humanity, we would not treat each other with anything less than the uttermost love and respect. And that is the great love that created Eve, she was the expression of the Father's love. A priceless treasure, indeed!

Absolutely, in you, as a woman, the Father created His *Magnum Opus*, His work of art—the grand finale of His creation masterpiece. Magnum opus is a Latin phase, meaning "great work." Referenced as the best, greatest, most popular, or renown work of an artist, indeed, magnum opus is the master piece of an artist's work.

In the Father's grand design for humanity, you are His magnum opus!

2

The Father's Dream

"Her children arise and call her blessed; her husband also,
and he praises her: 'Many women do noble things, but you
surpass them all.'" Proverbs 31:28-29 NIV.

AS A WOMAN, you are God's daughter, created as
the treasured joy of His own heart. With you, He will
bless the world. You are a gift—truly one of the
world's *greatest* gifts, and that is not an exaggeration.
God loved Adam and wanted to give him a gift that
would truly express His love toward him; you are that
incredible gift. You are the masterpiece of God's love
expressed to man.

However, as the effects of sin have settled over
our fallen world, the great gift God gave to mankind
has been diminished and the realization of the true
merit of women has been forsaken. In truth, the fall
did not *change* the value of women. No, it only
changed mankind's *perception* of the gift. Historically
that treasure has been undermined and stripped of its
true estimation. But regardless of the descending
glory of women in mankind's sentiment, God's design
has never altered.

After the fall, the Father looked at the woman He
had created with such great love and mourned for her
future, because He knew then all she would have to

endure through the release of sin on humanity. He was grieved that His beloved daughters would not be loved and valued as He had planned, but would, indeed, be dominated by the physically stronger male and treated with contempt.

In Genesis 3:16, the Father said, "Your desire will be for your husband, and he will rule over you" (NIV). He designed you to desire your husband, and with a few exceptions that is the case. Many have tried to use this scripture to indicate a "change" in God's purpose for women and the relationship between the sexes. However, that's a stretch, isn't it?

This scripture is not indicating a post-fall mandate for marriage, by no means! He was describing what the future would look like for them. Because He created women to desire men (most women do want to be married), they would still have that desire even after the fall. Yet now, due to wickedness, women would not be treated as equals, but dominated by the physically stronger male, abused and treated with contempt.

The depreciatory treatment women have had to endure is a result of sin and is a consequence of wickedness unleashed on humanity through the fall, it is not God's design nor His desire for His daughters or His sons. The Father saw the terrible struggle of His creation begin that day.

It was *never* the Father's plan for the strong to prey on the weak or for there to be any discord at all. He longed to see His created family in a loving relationship with mutual appreciation for one another. Through sin, the Father saw that His plan for an *equal friendship* between men and women would be ravaged by the pride and greed released by the fall, but *it is still His dream*.

God never planned on letting Satan win. Not for a moment did our loving Father give up on us. No, He would see His design for mankind carried out. He redeemed us. His miraculous plan of redemption (Genesis 3:15; Ephesians 3:3), will reestablish the peaceful, loving co-habitation between men and women He had as His original intent. God will have His way!

The Father's Dream Hasn't Changed

Jesus established a new way of thinking and living and tried hard to train His disciples to live by His kingdom principles. He knew if they could see themselves and each other as essential elements of His kingdom design, they would not grasp for an earthly throne.

In Mark 10:42-43, He described heaven's kingdom-mentality. "You know that those who are regarded as rulers of the Gentiles lord it over them, and their high officials exercise authority over them. Not so with you. Instead, whoever wants to become great among you must be your servant" (NIV).

The impulse of selfishness and greed, the desire to reign over others, even knocking them down if need be, is the result of sin. Yet, self*less*ness is the rule of God's kingdom and instinctively desires to raise others up. A self-centered heart wants all success for himself so he can feel superior. But a heart ruled by the kingdom of heaven finds joy in the successes of others in the kingdom.

Naturally, the same thinking must flourish in our dealings between men and women. Paul said, "...make my joy complete by being like-minded, having the same love, being one in spirit and of one mind. Do nothing out of selfish ambition or vain conceit. Rather, in humility *value others above yourselves*, not looking to your own interests but each of you to the interests of the others" (Philippians 2:2-4 NIV).

If we put this kingdom ideal above all other dogma and theology for marriage, there would be no divorce. Surely, there would be no need for this book, because husbands, preachers and the like would all seek to help women understand their value in Christ. Yes, they would fight *for* them, not *against* them—they would seek to raise them up so their voice and the wisdom they carry would be recognized and heard.

God designed love between a man and woman to be glorious and beautiful, never was His intention to make it something hard and legalistic. God designed us to love one another and He put in us a need to love as well, to protect and be protected and to join together with another that is our equal and truly, our *suitable* match. He designed us to need each other.

If woman was only taken from Adam's rib, men might lord it over women that he was her source of origin. But God, in turn, planned that every male since would come from woman. So, you see, our Father, in His infinite wisdom, planned us to need each other and He found this to be beautiful in His eyes. Men are the source of women and women are the source of men. We cannot do without each other—that is beautiful! Truly beautiful!

In 1 Corinthians 11:11-12, Paul describes the Father's design saying, "Nevertheless, in the Lord woman is not independent of man, nor is man independent of woman. For as woman came from

13

man, so also man is born of woman. But everything [including women] comes from God," (NIV emphasis mine).

Yet, the passages surrounding this beautiful scripture (1 Corinthians 11:3; 11:8), are examples Paul referenced of Jewish teachings, not Christian teachings, and have brought about much discord and error. To untangle this mess of Biblical misunderstanding, you first have to remind yourself that Paul did not know his writings would become a part of the Bible when he wrote them. Although no less anointed or inspired than the rest of the Bible, he was, indeed, writing letters to the churches he had founded and we know them as the Pauline Epistles.

When Paul references the Jewish beliefs of that day in 1 Corinthians 11:3, "The head of every man is Christ, the head of woman is man, and the head of Christ is God" (NLT) he uses the word *kephale,* which is interpreted to be *source* or *origin* 95% of the time it is translated in Scripture. Yet, for some reason here in this passage, the translators chose to interpret it as ruler or leader—head. However, it seems clear the interpretation of the word using *source* is more consistent with the rest of the message of Paul's letter. This lines up better when he later references 1 Corinthians 11:11-12 in which he again states our need for one another and God's original design being both male and female come from Him.

All throughout this letter, Paul taught the Corinthian church how they should behave toward non-Christians in public (Jews at temple). Previously in 1 Corinthians 10:18, Paul passionately shares his strategies for them to live as a witness to non-believers. In verses 23 and 24, He said that we "have the right to do anything—but not everything is constructive. No one should seek their own good, but the good of others" (NIV)

Though Paul was a free man, he chose to behave like a slave *to win others to Christ.* He said, "To the Jews I became like a Jew, to win the Jews. To those under the law I became like one under the law (though I myself am not under the law), so as to win those under the law." (1 Corinthians 9:19-20 NIV). And then Paul told the Corinthians to follow his example (1 Corinthians 11:1).

Paul did not stop in the middle of his message on evangelism and make a detour into a message on the inequality between men and women. Seen in light of his previous thoughts, we can see that his message toward the differing genders was not a truth to be recognized at all times, but was his advice to Christian families in *how to relate to Jewish families in public* so they could ultimately win them to Christ.

To clarify that they were only to live according to the Jewish traditional beliefs when they were among unbelievers in an effort to win them, he said, "But *among the Lord's people* [that's their sect of Christians or church], women are *not* independent of men, and men are *not* independent of women. For although the first woman came from man, every other man was born from a woman, and *everything comes from God*" (1 Corinthian 11:11-12 NLT emphasis mine).

The word "but" obviously means he's saying something opposite of what he had previously said. Like, hey, when you're in public do as the Jews do, but among ourselves we know that women and men are equal. This is Paul's firm belief. Everything he said previously was for the benefit of winning souls and not to be lived out amongst the believers.

Peter agreed in 1 Peter 3:7 he said, "In the same way, you husbands must give *honor* to your wives. Treat your wife with understanding as you live together. She may be weaker [physically] than you are, but she is your *equal partner* in God's gift of new life. Treat her as you should so your prayers will not be hindered" (1 Peter 3:7 NLT emphasis mine). In Christ, we are equal partners and should be honored as such.

Yes, God used Adam's rib to make Eve, but the creator and designer of women is not man, but God (1 Corinthians 11:12). Man can neither take credit for the idea of womankind or of their creation. For Adam and Eve were *both* made by God in the image of God, for the purposes of God's design (Genesis 1:27).

Fighting For the Value of Women

The most dangerous belief is believing you are better than others. Truly, by believing you are better than another race or gender you are endangering your own soul. Pride makes you vulnerable and opens the door to other dark devices of the enemy. Pride, especially religious pride, shields us from recognizing the fear and hatred we harbor. If we courageously look deeper at the reasons for our defensiveness towards others, we can deal with any hidden issues of insecurity we may have. Any belief system that protects fear is not from God, God does not give us fear or hate – if we entertain fear or animosity we join forces with the enemy, turning our back on the

Father.

It is clear that although Christ and Paul both tried very hard to influence their generations away from the poisonous beliefs against women, it remained still even in some of the different slants taken in Scripture as they were referenced and translated. Honestly, I love the Word of God. It is life to me, and I think it would be a very serious violation against it to slant it in a way that would devour or cause injury against any group of people. The Word of God is *His*, it belongs to God and should give an accurate account of His character; it should in no way characterize Him as being down on or against any one gender or race.

For centuries, such toxic beliefs against women have circulated through Christianity causing women and men to believe women are, indeed, second-class citizens. They are not and were not from the very beginning, and the bias against women has never been acceptable in God's eyes. It is time it came to an end.

Christ came to deliver women from the traditions of the enemy and lead them back to their original design. Paul reminded the Corinthians of Christ's revolutionary teaching, because it is truth as strong and as powerful as every truth God ever spoke to humanity. As followers of Christ, we need to follow His lead in everything, especially how we relate to other human beings—women are no exception.

Christian men should fight *for* women to know their true value, *not* against them, if for no other reason than it is a lie of the enemy and an attack against humanity. My husband was the first person who told people I was smart and over time he was able to convince even me that I was, in fact, a very intelligent person. We should all fight to convince each other of the greatness inside each of us—that's Christianity!

As Christians we should all fight even the slightest error in our beliefs that would wound young girls like my daughter, Cassandra, eroding their ability to know who they truly are in Christ. We should fight anything that would hinder them from confidently fulfilling the calling God has placed on their lives or any teaching presuming to misrepresent the heart of the Father by targeting young women with bias, hateful theology.

If we don't fight for truth, what inheritance are we giving our daughters? Is their inheritance to be one of confidence in their heavenly Father who loves them and values them, or one that cripples them and strips them of their purpose for living?

Satan's Afraid of You

In view of all the erroneous teachings against women throughout the centuries, often disabling or diminishing any witness they may have, you have to ask yourself, *Why would Satan even bother launching such an avalanche of attacks against women?*

In the media, I've frequently heard politicians bring up the *war on women* as if it is something that just began yesterday. This may come as a surprise to some, but there has always been a war on women. Truly, it is a war on humanity and heaven as well. It began at the fall and will continue until the end of this age. Experiencing highs and lows, women have always been victims of the forceful drive to terrorize and dehumanize. If the enemy can effectively diminish the humanity of women, he can more easily tempt men to commit atrocities against them.

Our world is experiencing a literal pandemic of violence against women and it will only increase until we, as a society, begin to recognize the egalitarian nature of women. Truly, men will continue to be in danger of sinking to the lowest depths of degradation and abuse toward women until they recognize them as equals and honor them accordingly.

In every war, women have been violated and used as a means of humiliating and terrorizing countries who've been subjugated. Yet, the levels of depravity we are seeing today in human trafficking alone are astronomical in comparison. Women are literally being hunted down and enslaved for profit. Sex-trafficking shows no signs of slowing down, no, quite the contrary. It is time that the church makes a stand for women! We need to demand that the body of Christ recognize their humanity or men will continue to fall prey to the divisive schemes of the enemy.

Truly, the enemy's attack against women is motivated solely by his fear of them. He is scared to death by the Father's prophetic sentence assigned against him. God foretold the power women would have over Satan and it's generated incredible fear through all of hell since. When God said, *"I will put enmity between you [Satan] and the woman, and between your offspring [seed] and hers; he [Jesus] will crush [strike] your head, and you will strike his heel"* (Genesis 3:15 NIV), He promised to crush Satan through the seed of the woman and that promise has continued to strike agonizing terror throughout the kingdom of darkness.

Indeed, Satan is absolutely terrified of women and has been since the fall. And we as women, must learn that through the power and authority we have in

Christ, we are more than equal to any war launched against us.

With Satan's fear rightly justified, I can tell you the realization of God's promised war has only just begun. We, as women, have only just barely begun to fulfill the promise of what is coming against the realms of darkness *through women*. The Father also promised through Joel in 2:28-29, "*Your sons and daughters will prophesy...In those days I will pour out my Spirit even on servants—men and women **alike**!*"

3

The Concubine's Legacy

"We must do something! So speak up!" Judges 19:30 NIV.

THE FIRST TIME I spoke at church I was twenty-four years old. It was Mother's day, my husband was the pastor and used the occasion as a reason to have me preach. He always felt I was called to preach and continuously urged me to do so. I can't say I did a good job of it, though. Honestly, I was a nervous wreck and was blessed to even get through it. However, the memorable moment of the day came *after* my sermon.

When I finished, I had walked only two steps off the stage and was met by a man who grabbed my arm and whispered in my ear, "I want you to know, I do not believe in women preaching." He was visibly angry.

At the time, I remember not being too shaken by the man. He was, after all, a very odd and cranky older man who really never gave me the slightest hint of loving the Lord. So, I tried very hard to disregard his comments to me that morning, but...

Later of course, the enemy got a hold of his words and spun them around and around in my head. Satan was trying to make me believe that I was doing something inappropriate or even sinful by preaching God's word.

Try as I might to wrestle the thought to the ground, it just kept coming up until at last I took it to the Lord. A few days later, I asked Him, "Why did you call me to preach if I am not supposed to?" I got no answer from Him until later that morning.

Walking past my Bible, which lay open on my table, I saw the pages flip as if caught in the breeze as I walked by it. I heard the Lord say, "Read it." So, I did.

My Bible was now turned to a little talked about passage in Judges. It was Judges 19—a mournful story about a nameless concubine.

In it, a Levite man from Ephraim had mistreated his concubine, and so she left him to return to her father's house in Bethlehem. Following her to Bethlehem, the Levite convinced her to return back home with him to Ephraim. As they were traveling back to Ephraim, they got as far as Gibeah and decided to stay the night in the center of town when an older gentleman who lived there passed by and offered his home to the weary guests.

As the night progressed and the men visited with each other, a gang of troublemakers gathered around the old man's house and started banging on the door. They demanded the old man give over the Levite man to them so they could have sex with him.

The old man objected vehemently and offered his virgin daughter and the Levite's concubine as a way of escape for the Levite. Yet, before they could refuse his offer, the Levite grabbed his concubine and shoved her out the door at the gang of men.

After raping the poor woman all night, the

demented beasts finally let her go in the early part of morning. Through what must have been tormenting agony, she managed to find her way back to the old man's house and collapsed on the threshold of the door. In some versions of the Bible, it is stated she left marks in the threshold where her fingers had dug into it.

In the morning, the Levite arose to leave. When he opened the door, he discovered his concubine laying on the doorstep. Giving her a nudge with his foot, he told her to "get up, it's time to get going," but she had died.

Taking her body home with him, he cut it up in to twelve pieces and had a piece sent to each tribe of Israel. As the ruthless crime was uncovered, the outrage grew over the atrocity that occurred in Gibeah.

At this point I felt flabbergasted and sat my Bible down and I asked the Lord, "Why did you have me read that?" He told me to keep on reading.

The Battle for the Value of a Woman

Forming an army of 400,000 men, the best soldiers from every tribe of Israel gathered at Gibeah and demanded someone pay for the awful crime that had taken place in their city, but the city refused to relinquish the men who had committed the heinous act. Indeed, instead of surrendering the men, they sent for an army from their tribe, the tribe of Benjamites and gathered 26,000 men to fight against the other tribes of Israel.

Encouraged by their overwhelming advantage against the Benjamites, the Israelites immediately sent troops in to fight against the tribe of Benjamin. That day, their advantage did them very little good and they lost 22,000 men.

At this point in the battle, you have to recognize the fact that the men who were lost in battle were not the Gibeahites or the Benjamites. No, the men that were lost were 22,000 men from Israel—the good guys, experienced swordsmen, military elite. These men were those who wanted to fight the injustice they had discovered and were willing that no such dreaded act be left unpunished amongst their countrymen. And yet, 22,000 of them were killed. They wept as they sought the Lord, asking, "Should we fight against our relatives from Benjamin again?" (Judges 20:23 NLT).

The Lord spoke to them, "Go out and fight against them." With a renewed sense of justice, they returned to fight the second day. Yet, again, they were met with disaster. Losing 18,000 more men.

Understandably, they were very distraught and returned to the Lord at Bethel, asking again if they were in the right and how they should proceed.

The Lord answered them and said, "Go! Tomorrow I will hand them over to you" (Judges 20:28).

That day, the Israelites ambushed the Benjamite army and drew them out of the city and God did give them the victory. Indeed, it was the tribe of Benjamin this time who lost over 25,000 men that day and the troublemakers were brought to justice.

After three days of battle, over 65,000 men lost their lives, all for ONE NAMELESS CONCUBINE!!

You see, to God the concubine had a name and He knew her quite well. She was valuable to Him. She was a precious treasure seeking to be loved in a cold world overwhelmed by the hatred and deception of the fall.

As she was tormented and attacked, she was not alone—God was with her! Her creator was with her, feeling every blow Himself. Everything they did to her that fateful night, everything her "husband" had done to her and every nasty destructive message launched at her, He felt. He bore it in Himself and all of it had become a heavy offense indeed.

In the gift of woman He gave to mankind, He imparted a great deal of His heart. The concubine was no exception. She, known only as the Levite's concubine in Scripture, was a treasure and dearly loved by her Creator.

God would have justice—justice for His own heart—as He saw His gift treated like refuse. 65,000 men died to bring justice to her—indeed, justice to humanity. His heart was heavy with the sin against the treasure He cherished so much, so God refused to make it easy for them—His heart needed restitution.

You see, your Father saw centuries into the future and He knew that someday you would be desperate to understand your true value in His sight. He wants you to know how highly He values you. He wants you and I to see that we matter to Him. He saw our value and refused to leave us without redemption.

God wants you to know that no matter what others have said or done, He will redeem the grossest atrocity and make you brand new. He is well able to take the daggers of your adversary and turn them into weapons for you to use against your enemy.

He can make you brand new!

Through His grace, your heavenly Father will

restore the bitter years of your life and release you to become the woman you've always dreamed you could be. Rebuke the trauma the enemy has released into your life. Take your life back and give it to God.

Surely, all hell has come against you because God loves you and values you. Give your heart to the Father and He will restore it, making it brand new. He will give you His life, for the life that has been stolen from you. Ask Him and He will. He can redeem you from any darkness attacking your soul and free you from its clutches. "He will make your innocence radiate like the dawn, and the justice of your cause will shine like the noonday sun" (Psalm 37:6 NLT).

Bathsheba was Raped

When we get to heaven and can ask both David and Bathsheba about their relationship, I believe many people will finally see the truth about Bathsheba's character. It's unfortunate that people would seek to pardon David's transgression in their minds by placing blame on Bathsheba.

According to the sermons I've heard, what we are expected to believe about Bathsheba was that she was a loose woman who bathed naked on her rooftop in order to seduce a king. She, once enticing him, got herself pregnant by him to scheme her way into the palace. Or at the very least, she, along with David, fell into an extramarital affair willingly. Hogwash!

First of all, bathing outside at the cool of the day was very common during that time period in that part of the world, and she was not naked, but robed as she bathed with servants who used special oils for cleansing and purifying treatments. She was in her own courtyard, possibly surrounded by a screen. Also, it was a common rule of decency in their world that as their regular hour of bathing took place, men were definitely not supposed to be peeping on them. It was taboo for men to use this as an opportunity to take advantage of women at this vulnerable time.

The fact that David was "walking around" at that time of day clearly indicates a willingness to commit an immoral act, even if it was just looking. It was a clearly understood and acceptable, normal way and time for baths to be taken. This was a part of an understood code of decency that was respected by everyone and was the respected bath time for women. Honoring societal codes of conduct meant not placing yourself where you could see the ladies bathing.

Contrary to popular teaching, Bathsheba, did not go willingly to the palace. Indeed, the scriptures say in 2 Samuel 11:4 (NASB), that David "took her" and "lay with her." The words used to describe what happened to Bathsheba at that time were "saw," "sent," "took her," "and lay with her" indicating what a fast paced and inhuman experience this was for her.

Was she human to David? Was she someone he even loved? No, David didn't love her; he lusted after her and he, taking advantage of his position, overwhelmed her with heartache. She wasn't a person to David, she was just another woman he had to have.

After David had intercourse with her, she left. Bathsheba chose to go back to her home. Surely, this shows she was not desiring sex with David, as she wanted to leave as soon as she was allowed. Had she not conceived a child because of the act, she would have probably never heard from David again. Yet, she was forced to contact him due to the child they'd conceived. Her message to David was not full of romantic phrases, but a simple blatant, "I am pregnant" (2 Samuel 11:5 NIV).

What happened to Bathsheba is what experts call power-rape, when someone uses their position of authority to force themselves on a woman. Or, what I consider to be "assisted rape," for she was brought in against her will by David's men. If she were to scream, who would come to her aid? David's men? No. She was imposed upon, and was not at all responsible for what happened to her. Bathsheba was targeted and brought to David, he had his way with her and then she left—how can anyone see romance in that?

When God acknowledged this sin through Nathan (2 Samuel 12:1-13), he did not at all accuse Bathsheba. But, unfortunately, she did bear the consequences and the child she carried lived only a few days. She went from being the wife of one man whom she loved, to becoming a part of a harem of wives of a man she barely knew. In 2 Samuel 11:26-27, Bathsheba was overcome by the news of her husband's death. The Greek word used to describe her mourning is not the regular word used, but *sapad*, which referred to "beating the breast."

After David had her husband Uriah killed (2 Samuel 11:27), the Word says David sent for her again and had her brought into the palace, but in the Greek the word used is *asap* which means *harvested*. What an aggressive word to use for such a moment, but, indeed, that is what he did—he harvested her. Far from a romantic affair, it was cold ruthlessness.

No, Bathsheba was not a co-conspirator, but another victim of a world that did not honor or respect the tremendous gift of love God gave mankind. She was imposed upon grievously. Just like we take the sunshine and fresh air for granted, women, too, have been taken for granted for centuries.

However, God showed me that Solomon's reign (1 Chronicles 29:22) was Bathsheba's blessing from Him. God wanted to make it up to her and chose her son over all of David's other sons to take His father's place, because she behaved honorably through a horribly dishonoring experience.

God sees and He feels deeply the wrongs that you have suffered, and will remain faithful to you—He will find a way to make it up to you. Never doubt His justice, just wait for it!

Gang Rape in India

While writing this book, I saw in the news the story of a young woman who was raped in Delhi, India. She went to her first American movie, *The Life of Pi*, with a male friend and never returned home. While on the public bus, she was gang-raped and sodomized, and died a few days later at the hospital. This incident sparked outraged all over the world and began a movement among women all over India to protest the treatment of women in their country.

But our protest shouldn't start at rape and death. It should start at the basic fundamental rights of women: to be honored and respected as equals. Until we are respected, there will always be incidents of rape and trafficking. Men will always treat women with rage and contempt as long as they are looked upon as less than themselves. Women's humanity will always be in question and they will be treated like sexual objects by a culture who is inundated with perversion.

The Church needs to be the first to declare the unequivocal equality of women in and out of the church and be willing to fight for them. We have the truth and it's time we made the truth matter and change the lives of women all over the world.

I Belong to Jesus!

I had a friend who was attending a Christian University with her husband. They were expecting their first child together. As with many college students they were strapped for cash, lived in a lower-level apartment and he worked nights to make ends meet. One night as she was alone, a man broke in through her window. She was asleep in her bed and he tried to rape her, but she screamed out, "I belong to Jesus! You can't have me!"

The man was literally thrown back and looked at her in unbelief. Several times he tried to lunge at her again, but she just kept screaming, "I belong to Jesus, you can't have me!" The man finally got frustrated and left.

What God says about you is the truth and what He has destined for your life, you will accomplish. The only thing that can stop Him is what you believe about yourself. And so, I ask you: do you know your true value? We are God's daughters, made by Him to enrich the world. We need to understand our true value. Because changing the way others think about us, starts with how we think of ourselves.

Your Father DOES NOT want you to be treated disrespectfully. He does not want you to be abused. That is NOT His will for you! He wants to restore you and heal you, and make you a showcase of His goodness and power!

We need to declare to the world, the church and to even to ourselves, "I belong to Jesus! Devil, you can't have me!"

4

Key to Revival: Galatian 3:28

"There is neither Jew nor Gentile, neither slave nor free, nor is there male and female, for you are all one in Christ Jesus" Galatians 3:28 NIV.

THE IMMENSE REVELATION in Galatians 3:28 is like an entire book in itself in regards to the earth-shattering power it possesses. Truly, it contains the keys to life's greatest blessings and happiness. Unfortunately, it seems like a book that's been lost on a shelf, forgotten and waiting for the bride of Christ to discover the depth of treasure it holds. Indeed, this scripture holds the power to release a massive, worldwide revival and transform the church as we know it.

When I read it, it makes me want to sing, "Red and yellow, black and white they are precious in His sight." But it's not a fluffy children's song. It's a stick of dynamite! If we will embrace it, this truth will completely rock our world. Literally!

The Father showed me what was truly meant by this scripture. He said, "*This is true revival. This is what My end-time bride will look like—what makes her without spot or wrinkle. This is what heaven looks like."*

When God looks at you, He sees Jesus—plain and simple. He does not see your race, sex or social standing—He sees His Son's blood covering you. To Him, we all look alike. Of course, He knows us each separately and intimately, but *through Christ, we are made equal.* He doesn't see race or sex—to Him it doesn't matter, and if we want to be like Christ, it won't matter to us either.

Beautiful Bride

How the Lord's bride treats women matters to Him—that is why He spends so much time talking about it. Seeing Galatians 3:28 manifest in our lives is important to Him because He knows the hindering power of pride and wants desperately to free us from it. For "God opposes the proud but shows favor to the humble" (James 4:6 NIV) and *He wants to pour out His grace and favor on all of us!*

The Lord's heart explodes with joy when His beloved seeks to please Him by loving without bias and building one another up. Yet, how deeply grieved He is when He sees His lovely bride allowing discrimination to be a part of their lives. Indeed, we show the world how to love every day and our love should exemplify His.

Racism, sexism and favoring the rich are not the way of God's Kingdom. When Christ talks about His bride being without spot or wrinkle (Ephesians 5:27), He is talking about a church that shows no partiality, and loves without hesitancy. This is what He's leading us to: to become His beautiful, spotless bride who loves as He loves.

In Luke 10:25-37, Jesus told the story of the good Samaritan who took such wonderful care of the man who'd been attacked on his way to Jerusalem, it showed those around him how they should be living. The priest and the Levite were known to be godly men, yet did nothing for the injured man. The Samaritans were hated by the Jews, yet Jesus made him the hero of His story, as he went out of his way to help the man recover from the attack. It was the Samaritan, not the Jewish leaders, who refused to walk away.

What Christ was trying to reveal through this parable was what truly mattered to Him. It doesn't matter to Him if you are a scholar, pastor or teacher, but that you are revealing the character of Christ through your actions. By loving without conditions, we reveal Christ on earth—we are bringing heaven to the world. People believe what we do much more than what we say, and to some, we may be the only Bible they will ever read.

When God Looks at You, He Sees Jesus!

But honestly, what does Galatians 3:28 really look like? It looks like equality. It looks like being absolutely treated as an equal with the same status and capabilities. We should not look at anyone and judge him or her to be inferior or to disqualify them by their race, gender or social status, nor value them by how much money they have. To do so would be to discriminate against them, as though God Himself created them to be inferior.

It is quite clear that Christ came to dismantle the

traditions of mankind and show us how to love in His church. Galatians 3:28 simply destroys all the man-made levels or sects of society and gives to each human being the gift of justice. Through Christ, the curse of the fall (or the curse of where you came from) is broken.

When you embrace the work of the cross, you are no longer a marginalized female, but you are one in Christ with His kingdom. *When God looks at you, He sees Jesus!*

Yet, racism and sexism are still prevalent in our churches, and sexism is even seen as pious, Godly behavior by some. Sadly, many times we turn a blind eye to the scripture in James that says, "If you give special attention and a good seat to the rich person, but you say to the poor one, 'You can stand over there, or else sit on the floor' well, doesn't this discrimination show that your judgments are guided by evil motives?" (James 2:3-4 NLT). We should ask ourselves the same question about sexism.

We need to think about and be reminded of the basic truths of Christ's mission—to liberate the captives. And *those who are held by the bondage of discrimination should especially find freedom in us, the church*. It should be our kingdom mission to see that they are raised up and encouraged to do the "greater works" Christ spoke about.

Azusa Street

One of my favorite historical revivalists is William J. Seymour. He was an African American preacher in the early1900s that God used to usher in the Azusa Street revival and help establish the Pentecostal movement. What I find so fascinating about him is his incredible hunger and humility.

Seymour and his family lived in abject poverty and suffered the many injustices of racism found in the south during that time. Yet, God used him to pour out His Spirit on this nation as he continually crossed race and gender barriers.

In 1905, Seymour moved to Houston, TX where he attended a Bible school led by Charles F. Parham who taught about the baptism of the Holy Spirit with the evidence of speaking in tongues. Seymour wanted to attend Parham's classes but, because of the segregation laws of the times, was forced to sit outside in the hallway and listen to Parham's teachings through an open door. He submitted himself to this humiliation because he was so desperate for God.

Moreover, though sexism was a hot issue in the church, he allowed himself to be led by many spiritual women. Indeed, it was through a woman, Lucy Farrow, that he first encountered the gift of praying in tongues and it was she who introduced him to Parham.

Throughout his ministry, Seymour continued to release women of all races into all forms of ministerial leadership. He saw firsthand the spiritual impact women had on the meetings they led and valued the anointing on their lives.

Even though women greatly helped usher in the Azusa revival, it is unfortunate that, as the Pentecostal movement became more organized, women were assigned mainly subordinate roles. Sadly, the movement split along lines of race.

Even after the outbreak of revival, Seymour

continued to experience racial and gender bias by Spirit-filled Christians, which led him to believe that *the breaking down of the race and gender barriers was a more sure sign of revival than that of speaking in tongues.* Truly, this is a very important and powerful truth and one that should stay in our focus as we endeavor to move into greater realms of revival.

"Key to Church Growth?"

Loren Cunningham is another person of faith I dearly admire. He's the author of one of my favorite quotes. He says, "When God begins a dramatic work of His Spirit, women are often in the forefront."[1] He has done much to promote women in ministry and has empowered, encouraged and sent women of all ages and races all over the world.

In Cunningham's book, *Why Not Women*, co-authored with David Hamilton, he quotes Dr. Yonggi Cho of South Korea who leads the world's largest church. Dr. Cho was asked what the key to his church's growth was. He said simply, "Release your women!"[2]

Cho started his church at the home of Choi Ja-shil, a strong woman of faith and his associate in ministry. He said his church did not have the breakout growth until he allowed the anointed women of his congregation to take leadership roles and to preach and teach the people. It was then they experienced massive growth and power.

Personally, Dr. Cho had no problem with women preaching. But in order to release them in their calling, he had to overcome the traditions of generations. The funny thing about traditions is they seem so normal because we are so used to them. Little more than a century ago, slavery was thought to be normal and some even taught it as Bible truth.

Of course now, such a short time later, we know slavery to be one of the most shameful and decadent issues in our history. Was it right then, but wrong now? No, it was wrong then, too. And sexism is no different.

Some of the bias in the church today has its origins, not in God's Word, but in man-made traditions. Truly, if we want God's Spirit, yet we don't like the vessel it is coming through, we don't really want His Spirit after all, do we? If we are hungry for Him, we will toss out our traditions and embrace God's blessing.

Truly, God beams with pride when His children are willing to embrace the full measure of Galatians 3:28. For anywhere women, the poor or minorities are protected and treated as equals, God shows up. What joy and freedom we flow in when we allow our hearts to love unconditionally, without bias; what supernatural power we unleash as we embrace the liberty of this compelling scripture.

So, dear friends, if you hunger for more of God, embrace Galatians 3:28! If you want God's glorious miracle-working power evident in your life, remember Galatians 3:28!

Galatians 3:28 is simply and truly LOVE! And God IS love!

(1) *Why Not Women* by Loren Cunningham and David Hamilton 24

(2) *Why Not Women* by Loren Cunningham and David Hamilton 67

5

Liberty to the Captives

"Our Father in heaven, hallowed be your name, your kingdom come, your will be done, on earth as it is in heaven" Matthew 6:9-10 NIV.

THE CROSS SETS things right.

The cross bore the shame and sin of the fall of mankind and revealed the kingdom of heaven to the human race. God's heavenly kingdom would not dominate or cast aside any human, regardless of race, gender or position. Indeed, God will pour out His Spirit on every human being who will receive Him. Jesus emancipated humanity and declared to the Earth, "The kingdom of God is already among you" (Luke 17:21 NIV).

Christ presented us with a new way of thinking: *the mindset of heaven*. He taught us to pray to the Father, "May your will be done on earth, as it is in heaven" (Matthew 6:10 NLT), literally calling down the mindset of the kingdom to invade and overtake the earth.

When we ask the Father to manifest the reality of heaven on earth, we are asking for the love and acceptance that heaven enjoys to come and invade the church, the world and our hearts. We are asking for the traditions of man, the lies of history and the hatred and fear of generations to be washed away by the cross of Christ. This prayer, the *Father's prayer*, reveals a new existence and a new way of thinking and living to the earth.

Indeed, that includes the lies told against women, which must be exposed and *God's truth about women* be instituted in our hearts and minds. So, we should then be asking ourselves, "How does *heaven* treat women?" The nearest example we have is the life of Christ.

What did Jesus say about women when He lived on the earth? How did Jesus treat women? Or better yet, what didn't Jesus teach us about ourselves?

Jesus challenged the world He lived in with the truth. He foresaw His sacrifice on the cross and knew it would bring liberty to men and women alike! He knew the cross would send the world reeling, but would bring about the ultimate liberation of an entire gender—that 50% of His bride would ultimately be set free from the bonds and chains of tradition's lies against them.

Jesus, our Savior, died to liberate you and me. He died to liberate both men and women—it was a part of the package, an essential element to equip the church. So, why do women continue to allow their liberty to be stripped away from them?

Think about it. Paul was speaking to the Corinthians in 2 Corinthians 11:19-20, but he was talking to women and men both when he said, "After all, you think you are so wise, but you enjoy putting up with fools! *You put up with it when someone enslaves you*, takes everything you have, takes advantage of you, takes control of everything, and slaps you in the face" (NLT emphasis mine).

For centuries, many women have allowed themselves to be devalued and believed they were serving God by doing so.

Previously, I wrote about the first man who told me I couldn't walk in the calling God put on my life. But, I have yet to tell you of all the countless women who thought that simply by using the gifting and anointing on my life, I was in rebellion to God.

The enemy will try any contemptible lie he can to keep you from doing what you are called to do. He will wrap a morsel of truth around a bundle of lies and call it wisdom and try to make it law.

Should we let him stop us?

Would you let Satan stop you from defending your children if they were in danger or your church if it needed your help? Why let him limit you? Why allow him to take up space in your mind with his debunked theories of womanhood when the Word of God clearly states that you were called for such a time as this. *"I will pour out my Spirit upon all people. Your sons and DAUGHTERS will prophesy. Your old men will dream dreams, and your young men will see visions. In those days I will pour out my Spirit even on servants—**both men and women alike**!"* Joel 2:28 NLT (emphasis mine).

Christ died to set women free from the intolerable burdens they were never meant to bear so they could take their place in His kingdom on earth without reservation or excuse. Why, then, would we ever allow ourselves to become enslaved again by the traditions of mankind and reproach ourselves for our lack of compliance to the indoctrination the church has handed out to us as spiritual food?

Why would we disregard the freedom Christ died

to give us? Why would we throw away the humanity He handed us? It is His gift to us; our freedom through Christ is our inheritance from Him. He came to set women free.

God, our Father, has designed and planned for you to take your place in the battle for the kingdom—to do the greater works of the kingdom! When you embrace the work of the cross, you are no longer a marginalized female, but you are one in Christ with His kingdom. Remember: *when God looks at you, He sees Jesus!*

When you triumph over mankind's opinion of you, you triumph for the kingdom of heaven.

Half-built House

The Holy Spirit showed me a vision years ago of a great, towering building. The structure had a foundation and floors on every level, but had completed walls on only two sides and no roof. In the building, there was a great multitude of men and women working as if they were oblivious to the conditions of the building they were in. They were simply unaware of their terrible lack and the vulnerable situation it put them in.

I asked God about the vision. He said, "My house is not yet finished and it will remain unfinished and vulnerable to the enemy until the women take their rightful place in My house."

I found it peculiar He did not say the women should be *given* their rightful place, but He said they must *take* their place. Unfortunately, there is still a great deal of misogynist thinking in the church amongst women against women. Indeed, God never said it would be easy and truly, the difficulties we face build us into the strong women we need to be to rally for our King.

My Journey to Freedom

For years as my husband and I pastored, I didn't realized that I was sexist against myself. Just for pure enjoyment, I used to write up little Bible studies, but didn't intend do anything with them. One day, my husband was struggling with what sermon he should preach the following Sunday and I suggested that he use one of my Bible studies. So, you guessed it—the following Sunday he preached a message I had received from the Lord.

I honestly thought he would appreciate my help, but later that day he told me how he felt about it. He said, "This is wrong, Victoria! If God has given you a message, you should be the one to preach it!" Well, that was the end of that and the beginning of what eventually became my ministry.

My husband, Steve, was, from that moment on, very passionate about what God was doing and saying through me and he did whatever was within his power to see me fulfill the call on my life. He fought many battles, promoted me to anyone who would listen and pushed, pushed, pushed me to pursue ministry and he has not let up.

From that moment until this, he has been very zealous about seeing women use their ministry giftings. It was Steve, not I, who pushed for me to have a ministry. He literally developed it and God brought other wonderful men of God into my life to encourage it once he had.

Years later, Steve began working for Francis Frangipane. One day, he came home from work with a stack of papers that I recognized as *my* Bible studies. He had sneaked my writings out of the house and took them to Francis. He came home quite proud of himself and said with a Cheshire-cat grin on his face, "Francis wants to publish your book!"

Steve knew me too well. He knew I was too shy and self-critical to show them to Francis myself, because I dearly valued Francis' opinion of my writing. So, Steve was not going to take the chance of me chickening out and refusing to let him take my writings to Francis, so he did it without me knowing.

As the book was being published, Steve worked to set up my ministry. He even named it himself. His passion is truly for the kingdom—to see liberty released among the saints. And he doesn't take no for an answer; he just prays it through!

You see, friend, I was, without realizing it, apologizing for the calling on my life. My husband understood that and fought hard to get me to see that what God had placed in me was truly valuable so I would use it.

Holy Spirit told me, "Never apologize for the calling on your life!" It is insulting to Him. He obviously knew I was a woman when He called me. It was easy for me to make excuses for the calling on my life, because I was so shy. Fear kept me in bondage until I determined to break its power over my life. But it wasn't easy...

I remember the first meeting I spoke at outside our church. I had been asked to speak at a women's Aglow meeting in a nearby town. Their scheduled speaker could not make it and they asked if I would fill in. I was so terrified. I said yes, but asked if my husband could speak instead of me and I offered to sing and pray instead.

Those poor ladies. I was so nervous my singing was probably the worst it's ever been. When Steve's message was over, he called me up to the front and announced to them, "Victoria is going to come now to pray and prophesy over your life." Now, you have to understand, I had never prophesied over anyone in public before.

Obediently, I walked sheepishly to the front of the room and positioned myself in front of the line of women Steve had organized for me. But then, he suddenly decided that they were all too close to the front row of chairs and might hit them when they "fell out under the Spirit's power," as he'd said they would.

As the line of women moved forward, I stood frozen in place as they all passed me and now I was standing behind them facing the back of the room in the opposite direction. I literally had to tell myself to move!

I walked around to the front of them again and steadied myself to pray. Beginning timidly, I began to pray and of course everything that Steve said would happen, happened. The power of God hit the place and all the women were touched by God.

It was wonderful, but, oh, what a battle!

If it had not been for Steve, I would not have attempted anything like that on my own. I was so shy, I needed his encouragement, and honestly, I have to say, I needed his pressure, without which I would have chickened out.

In order to see the treasure in women released, we

will have to fight for them. For, like myself, many women need help. Since I walked this path, it is a burden on my heart that other women be released to follow the Lord's leading and am now speaking out for them. I long to see women live in the freedom and liberty Christ purchased for them.

Truly, I believe there are many other men and women like my husband in the church. They will, like Jesus, stand and fight for women to be released and used powerfully in the kingdom—to see men and women walk equally in their callings and giftings. Without this battle for the destiny of women, the unity of the Father's house will remain compromised.

We, as a church, must stand vehemently against any and all opposition against the *whole* kingdom of heaven coming to the earth. It must be released through all of us—men and women *alike*!

6

As it is in Heaven

"He has sent me to comfort the brokenhearted and to proclaim that captives will be released and prisoners will be freed" Isaiah 61:1 NLT.

IT IS UNFORTUNATE that some men who I greatly esteem do not have equal respect for me solely because I am a woman. Their regard for me is limited, not by what I do or how I minister, but it would seem I am handicapped in their eyes simply because of my gender.

Jesus came to the earth to break the gender-bias that was held by the church during His day, yet it seems, though many accepted His ministry, they ignore the example He set for them. Indeed, He realigned women with the kingdom of heaven, positioning us to receive the Spirit's outpouring for the last days.

Jesus' mind was engulfed by His heavenly perceptions, and He imparted all of His Father's concepts, beliefs and actions to humanity. He lived His life on earth as an example of the prayer He taught us to pray to our Father. His life's breath was, "Your Kingdom come soon. May your will be done on earth, as it is in heaven" Matthew 6:10 NLT.

It was Christ's passion to see the model of His

Father's kingdom become the way of life for His followers on the Earth. "As it is in heaven!" are just five little words that come down like a hammer on our past traditions and mindsets.

My grandma use to make us all pray the Lord's prayer together before family meals—it was very important to her. Yet, I do not think she had any real idea of the tremendous power of this amazing prayer. For simply and truly, Jesus was calling forth all of the riches of heaven, its wealth of love and acceptance, to come and be made manifest in humanity on earth. His disciples ask Him to teach them how to pray, so He taught them to pray in accordance with His Father's will to be made manifest in their lives.

In an encounter I had with the Lord, He showed me His home in heaven. I have only seen heaven a few times, but in one particular encounter, I was so completely overpowered by the overwhelming feelings of the acceptance I felt in heaven. I literally did not realize how much oppressive rejection we live with every day here on earth. My mind and soul felt rejuvenated and restored by the penetrating sense of acceptance—it consumed me. I felt truly welcomed, understood, and celebrated. So, I can say with absolute certainty, something we should already realize: *there is no gender bias in heaven*!

As I came out of the encounter, my family could tangibly feel the acceptance of heaven. As I shared with them all I had seen, the essence of heaven's reception filled our home.

The love that is expressed in heaven is truly unconditional and is what our heavenly Father wants for us here in this world—in this life. "As it is in heaven" is what God wants for us and that is how He wants us to live—treating people with the respect and esteem of heaven. That is why Jesus was so passionate about heaven's kingdom possessing Earth's realm.

Truly, as Christ lived, He became a voice for anyone who was thought to be unacceptable or undervalued by earth's societal scale. Why? Because it was directly opposed to the Father's way in heaven and it stood in the way of the kingdom of God coming to earth!

One of the most prevalent attitudes Jesus fought hard against while on earth was the belief that women were inferior or second class. Jesus knew women and men were equal and this belief put Him in direct conflict with the religious leaders of the day. "Haven't you read," he replied, "that at the beginning the Creator 'made them male and female,' and said, 'For this reason a man will leave his father and mother and be united to his wife, and the two will become one flesh.' So they are no longer two, but one flesh. Therefore what God has joined together, let no one separate" Matthew 19:4-6 NIV.

Contrary to what is often taught about the Lord's conduct toward women, He accepted women into His ministry and had many women disciples as well: Mary Magdalene, Mary, the mother of Jesus, Mary Salome, Martha, sister of Lazarus, Miriamne, sister of Phillip, Arsinoe,[1] Susanna, and Joanna (Luke 8:1-3). Jesus lived His life as an example of how we were to relate to each other as human beings. He broke taboos, rules and laws in His conduct toward the women He came in contact with—the Word records the many incidents in His life where He openly empowered women, which was against the Jewish teachings and customs of the times.

Jesus allowed women to travel with Him, they were a part of His inner circle and were His disciples—He related with women as His equals (Matthew 27:55-56; Luke 8:1-3; Luke 10:38-42; John 2:5; John 4:4-26). Jesus did not teach inequality between the genders, He taught us to honor others as more important than ourselves and, in doing, so we would discover that is what truly make us great, not our race or gender (Mark 10:43). Love was much more important to Him than law (John 13:34).

Jesus came to purify the attitudes of humanity and start a revolution of love.

His goal was and is to cleanse us from any attitude which did not further the advance of the kingdom of heaven in our lives. Bias against women comes in squarely against God's love and is in stark contrast to the acceptance of heaven. Therefore, it is of paramount importance that we allow the Lord to purge us of any ideology that limits the manifestation of heaven in us.

Beliefs that limit women's ability to exemplify spirituality are corrupt social practices that have been accepted and advanced by the church. This is just the opposite of what Christ worked for.

Indeed, Jesus wanted the church, *His church*, to lead the world in displaying the example He set and break down the barriers against women and anyone who suffered under the weight of rejection and abuse. We were given the assignment and responsibility to *love with equality all* God's children.

Women are NOT Property

For centuries in America, we've felt the depravity of slavery and its horrendous effects on humanity. As a society, we have recognized the iniquity of slavery. Yet, it takes a lot for us to even acknowledge that fifty-percent of humanity has had to endure slavery for thousands of years.

Indeed, wives and daughters were considered to be the property of their husbands and fathers throughout history. As *"property"* women were expected to not only serve men, but to even derive feelings of self-worth from their acts of servitude to the men in their lives.

In John 8:3-11, we see how the men of the Lord's time thought nothing of exploiting a woman to try and catch Jesus in error. While Jesus taught the people, the religious leaders brought a woman who'd been caught in the act of adultery before Him. The word *brought* is a polite word to describe their inhuman treatment she experienced that day.

The trap was set. You see, the law states in Deuteronomy 22:22, "If a man is found sleeping with another man's wife, both the man who slept with her and the woman must die" (NIV). It wasn't the sin that inflamed the religious leaders, but that another man's *property* had been violated.

However, in the law it states that if the young woman was not engaged, then the man who had violated her had only to pay her father fifty shekels, then he would be allowed to marry her and neither of them would have to be killed in that instance. In that instance, she was no man's wife, so it was *okay* in the eyes of their law, as long as the father is reimbursed for his loss. (Deuteronomy 22:28-29).

Deuteronomy goes on to say that if a woman is even pledged to a man to be married and is raped, she must be stoned if she was raped in town, because that would mean she did not scream out for help and is therefore guilty of allowing another man's property to be violated, which was considered an act of "folly" on her part. Of course, if the woman is raped in the country (where her screams could not be heard), then only the violating man has to be stoned (Deuteronomy 22:23-27).

If a woman is only an object, a man's conscience has no regard for her quality of life.

For centuries, women, as property, could not own property, vote or earn an income. Their only recourse was to become someone's wife, remain a burden to their family, become a prostitute or simply starve—there were no other choices for them.

So, on the day Jesus met the woman caught in adultery, you can imagine the key religious teachers of the law dragging a poor, despondent, emotionally numb woman to Jesus. To further shame her they forced her to face the crowd of people while they tested Him. *They wanted to see if Jesus would stick up for her, or obey the law.*

"What do you say?" the Pharisees demanded of Him (John 8:5 NIV). Jesus refused to answer them, and bent down to write in the sand.

I can imagine the pity and sorrow Jesus felt for the woman who stood before Him. He knew full well she was being used as a pawn to trap Him. But, imagine His feelings toward the Pharisees, as He was gutted by their obvious corruption—they thought so much of themselves and their own piety and very little of the woman they held in contempt. Jesus knew it, and so refused to even acknowledge their nefarious behavior toward another human being.

Finally, "When they kept on questioning him, he straightened up and said to them, *'Let any one of you who is without sin be the first to throw a stone at her'*" (John 8:7 NIV).

As they walked away one by one, it seems they were able to see the contemptible condition of their own hearts as Jesus revealed their soul's true condition to be equal to the poor, wretched woman they wanted Jesus to kill. In redirecting their focus on to themselves, Jesus validated the woman's humanity as being equal to theirs.

Jesus wasn't caught as they had hoped, and was able still to aid the woman against the attack of the religious leaders, showing them how shameful their behavior toward this woman was. He treated her, not as property, but as someone who needed His protection in spite of her sin. Jesus saw her worth as more valuable than the *law* that had been violated. He saw her, not as property that had been desecrated, but as a daughter of His Father, created in His Father's image.

Jesus went even further and contrary to Jewish law, spoke directly to the woman in front of a crowd of onlookers. He asked her, "Woman, where are they? Has no one condemned you?"

"No one, sir," she said.

"Then neither do I condemn you," Jesus declared. 'Go now and leave your life of sin'" (John 8:10-11 NIV).

As Jesus made His judgment of the situation, remember that He spoke only what His heavenly

Father spoke. "For I did not speak on my own, but *the Father who sent me commanded me to say all that I have spoken*" (John 12:49 NIV). It was the Son and our Father who chose this situation to reveal to humanity: women are *not property*, but are, indeed, human beings created in the image and the likeness of God.

Twisting Truth

Our Father created His law through Moses to be a help to the Israelite nation. Yet, with just a little twisting of the mind, it was used as a weapon of destruction. But, through the situation with the woman caught in adultery, Jesus was able to show that women matter more than the law.

Jesus showed us that people were more important than the law when He said, "The Sabbath was made for man, not man for the Sabbath" (Mark 2:27 NIV) and He lived His life displaying this truth. He taught repeatedly that people were more valuable than religious rules and regulations have made them appear. Indeed, He offended the lawmakers in order to defend women.

Again, the Pharisees confronted Jesus in Matthew 19:3-9 about yet another passage from Deuteronomy and asked, "Is it lawful for a man to divorce his wife for any and every reason?" (Deuteronomy 24:1 NIV). He spoke up for women and reminded them of the Father's original design for men and women in Genesis.

"'Haven't you read,' He replied, 'that at the beginning the Creator 'made them male and female,' and said, 'For this reason a man will leave his father and mother and be united to his wife, and the two will become one flesh? So they are no longer two, but one flesh. Therefore what God has joined together, let no one separate.'"

"'Why then,' they asked, 'did Moses command that a man give his wife a certificate of divorce and send her away?'"

"Jesus replied, 'Moses permitted you to divorce your wives because your hearts were hard. **But it was not this way from the beginning**. I tell you that anyone who divorces his wife, except for sexual immorality, and marries another woman commits adultery'" (Matthew 19:4-9 NIV emphasis mine).

When determining our value as women and our role in marriage, we must continually come back to the Creator's original design for us. Knowing the Pharisees had been deceived by their hardness, *Jesus turned their focus back to the Father's original design, not Moses' allowances for their hard hearts.*

What a humiliating shock it must have been to them to be told they were made equal to the gender they despised so much. He called them *one flesh* with the women they believed mattered less than the cattle in their fields.

It makes me laugh thinking how they must have groaned when Jesus reminded them of the origin of women, which was Adam's own flesh (Genesis 2:23). That is why Paul said in Ephesians 5:29, "No one ever hated his own flesh, but nourishes and cherishes it, just as Christ does the church."

Jesus came to bring the values of His heavenly kingdom to the earth and openly displayed it, attracting the fire of the religious. Jewish men were proud of their manhood, yet, Jesus was quite happy to break down the walls of arrogant gender-bias that separated mankind.

Every morning in Judaism, a man began his day with a thanksgiving prayer to God as follows; "Praise be to God that he has not created me a gentile; praise be to God that He created me not a woman; praise be God that he has not created me an ignorant man" (Menahoth 43b).[2]

In essence, they started everyday cursing the women they shared their lives with and believed their behavior to be exceedingly pious, respected by God. In essence, they were depriving women of their equal inheritance as the treasured creation of their Father.

Jesus took the curse of the fall on Himself, and gave us back the authority and dominion we'd lost. Establishing the governmental rule of heaven on the earth, He restored for us the joy we had in each other. Clinging to the cross, we can, once again, reign together with our humanity and value restored and live as God had intended (Galatians 3:13). Through the eyes of Love we see perfectly!

Paul said in Galatians 3:26-29, "For ye are all sons of God, through faith, in Christ Jesus. For as many of you as were baptized into Christ did put on Christ. There can be neither Jew nor Greek, there can be neither bond nor free, there can be no male and female: for ye all are one man in Christ Jesus. And if ye are Christ's, then are ye Abraham's seed, heirs according to promise" (KJV). Hallelujah!

It's interesting that Paul said there can be no differences in Christ, meaning: equality is a part of our salvation and inheritance Christ died to give us. As followers of the Lamb, as children of our God, we are all equal in the kingdom of heaven and accepted into the Beloved. There can be no prejudices in Christ. Those inclinations must be fought against as much as greed, selfishness and any other sin.

Jesus Launched Women into Ministry

In John 4:7-26, Jesus met a Samaritan woman at the well of Jacob and asked her for water. As she served Him, He revealed to her Who He was. He met the need of her heart, delivering her of her shame and set her heart aflame with His love!

Knowing full-well she would share the great news of the Messiah, Jesus did not stop her from sharing it as He had done with others on all other occasions (Matthew 12:16). In His knowing silence, He started the first woman's ministry and many Samaritans believe because of her testimony of Him.

His disciples were of course shocked, because, again, Jesus broke the rules: He spoke to a woman publicly, taught her theology and, to make things worse in their eyes, she was a Samaritan.

According to Jewish teachings, He was not supposed to talk to a woman or a Samaritan and He was definitely not supposed to teach her theology. But Jesus hated all those *anti-heaven* rules! So, He not only talked with her, He turned her into an evangelist! He super-charged her with the acceptance from heaven, then stood back and watched while she brought a harvest of souls to Him.

What is interesting about the Samaritan woman Jesus chose is that she had previously been married *five times*. Her past was uncovered, yet, she was unashamed in the eyes of the Beloved; she was washed cleaned from the contempt of society.

Through *His eyes*, she saw herself only as the accepted of heaven and wanted the world to experience her joy!

I have heard so many Christians chastise divorcees with Malachi 2:16, "'For I hate divorce!' says the LORD, the God of Israel!" But the reason God hates divorce is because of its abhorrent treatment to the *woman* being divorced. For, "'To divorce your wife is to overwhelm her with cruelty,' says the LORD of Heaven's Armies" (NLT).

Understand that the women of this era were *never* allowed to divorce their husbands, for any reason. No, indeed, that was a "privilege" reserved only for the male sex, and use it they did. For any reason, a man could divorce his wife and keep her dowry, children and any possessions she had, leaving her destitute.

The Samaritan woman came to the well alone that day, and not while the other women of her village were getting water. No, she was a *rejected* woman who was divorced, who had been past from man to man. She was the utter explanation of Malachi 2:16; she'd been treated cruelly by the men in her life.

So, the women of her time were basically forced by society and by the law into marrying simply for survival. Then, for whatever reason the husband could cast her aside and her only hope then was to be picked up by another man. She was cast off and left to the mercy of men who did not value her except as an object of property to be owned and used. Sadly, wives could be treated horrendously by their husbands, beaten or killed and the law completely supported the man's actions.

The Father in heaven mourned for the plight of

His daughters and asked, "Who will help My daughters? Who will be their voice? Who will offer them another way?"

Jesus.

And so He did.

Jesus was never tempted to live His life according to the world's standards, for His goal was to redeem mankind. He redeemed us through the cross, but also through the examples He showed us in His own life. He lived His life to reveal the mindset of heaven to earth. His hope was that we as His bride would eventually learn these principles as well and manifest them through the way we treat each other.

We can't pick and choose which principles we'd like to live by. No, if we want to be His disciples and represent His kingdom, we must abide by the laws of heaven which are faith, hope and love: *Faith* to live a life that would transform the lives of others, *Hope* in the cross of Christ that separates light and darkness, and the *Love* of a very merciful Father who wants to draw us into Himself and make us His own.

(1) Credited to R. Judah b. Elai (c. AD 150) in Tos Berakoth 7:18 and Jer Berakoth 13b; and to R. Meier (c. AD 150) in Bab Menahoth 43b.

(2) Wilhelm Schneemelcher, ed., translation by R. McL. Wilson, New Testament Apocrypha: Gospels and Related Writings (Louisville: John Knox Press, 1992), pp. 313-326. The First Apocalypse of James. Also, Matthew 27:55-56, 61; John 19:25-27 (women at the cross); Matthew 28:1-11; Mark 16:1-9; Luke 24:1-13; John 20:1, 10-18; (women visiting the tomb); Mark 15:40-47 (women at burial) Luke 8:1-3 (women disciples) Luke 23:49 (women friends) John 11:1-44 (Mary and Martha); John 20:16 (Mary Magdalene recognizes Jesus) Acts 1:14 (at Pentecost); Acts 18:26 (woman disciplining Paul); Romans 16:1-15 (Paul promotes women ministers); 1 Corinthians 16:19 (woman ministering with Paul); Colossians 4:15; Philemon 1:2 (woman pastors/leaders).

·

7

Release My Daughters

"Jesus traveled about from one town and village to another, proclaiming the good news of the kingdom of God" Luke 8:1-3 NIV.

IN THE YEAR 2000, I experienced a commissioning encounter with the Lord that became a focus for my future ministry. In it, the Lord laid me out and shook me to my core. He said, "*You will champion for my women!*"

He continued... "*Soon I will release black men, and then I will release the women.*"

Only months after receiving this word from the Lord, I realized I was expecting my youngest child, CailieEllen. The nine months I carried her were very difficult. In fact, it was the most difficult pregnancy of all my four children.

At that time, we were at Francis Frangipane's church and, although the Lord had told me years before that my fourth child would be a girl, for a long time there had only been boys born at his church. Francis used to remark about the trend of male births, "God is doing something masculine at our church." But, God told me that all of that would change beginning with CailieEllen's birth.

All during my pregnancy with her, I had numerous

dreams that I gave birth to a little blonde girl who was mentally handicapped. I kept it to myself, not wanting to give way to the fears that tried to take hold of my heart.

I had terrible back pain while pregnant with her and went several times to receive prayer for it. But every time I went for prayer for my back, the people praying for me would end up praying for the life of my child as if they were sensing an impending attack against her.

When it came time for me to deliver my child, it seemed we were taken up in a whirlwind of confusion. My regular doctor was not available and we were being cared for by another doctor who was very cruel. He insisted on inducing labor to the point that he gave me an over dose of medicine that made it impossible for me to give birth naturally. CailieEllen was born by caesarian section and it was then we discovered the umbilical cord was wrapped around her neck three times. With other complications involved, she would have most likely been born with a mental handicap, as I had dreamt, if she would have come naturally.

After she was born and safe with us, I shared my dreams with my husband and he then told me he had had the same dreams and fears. Others, including Francis, told us later God had urged them to pray for CailieEllen, that He had warned them her life was in jeopardy—the enemy was trying to destroy her life.

The Lord showed me CailieEllen was a prophetic manifestation of the change God was bringing to His church. Until that time, only boys were born at our church. However, after CailieEllen was born, it switched to being primarily girls born there. Through the births of these baby girls, the Lord revealed to me that even though the enemy would try to launch an attack against His daughters, God would have His way and the girls would be saved and flourish.

"For My daughters," the Father is saying, "I will deliver the promise of Joel (Joel 2:28) to My church and an army of My mighty warrior women will arise!"

The first part of the commissioning word He gave me in 2000 was that He would release black men and they would come to the forefront. Say what you will about the outcome of the 2008 election of our nation's first black president, but you have to admit black men through this time have come to a new forefront in popular society. Through the example of this word's fulfillment, we can be further encouraged that God will keep the second part of this word. He will, indeed, release His daughters!

The Whole Pie

At the end of 2013, the Lord showed me a vision of myself and another man who I did not know. The Lord stood before us with one pie in His hands. He asked both the man and myself, "*Do you want a piece of this pie?*"

I answered immediately, "Yes, Lord. I want a piece."

Suddenly, the man beside me snapped at the Lord, "NO! Don't give her any pie, Jesus! She's a woman!"

I was shocked, but the Lord was not. It seemed He had anticipated the man's response and calmly turned to me and handed me the entire pie. The man got nothing from the Lord that day.

Fast forward to 2014, the Lord spoke to me and

said, "*Victoria, there is no greater day to be a woman in ministry!*"

I believe these visions stand as a declaration of the day we are in. We've come to the season of the kingdom of heaven—sexism and greed have no place in it. Ministries will grow seemingly overnight, while some will harden to the plans of the Lord and dwindle. It is a heart issue, and will be judged solely by the Lord. Sexism will no longer be tolerated by our Father.

It has become my passion, as well as my delight, to see women move to the forefront of ministry. It gives me great joy to see them stand in the wisdom and confidence of the Lord and to gather around the other women as they walk out their completed prophetic destiny in Christ.

Dr. Yonggi Cho

Dr. Paul (David) Yonggi Cho, pastor of the largest church in the world, said in an interview with Felicity Dale, "You in the West will never see a move of God until you use your women."[1]

Pastor Cho's church has grown through much prayer, but also through the vital role women have played in it. Dr. Cho first released his mother-in-law into ministry at his church, then later, thousands more have joined her.

His church is now over 800,000 strong and two-thirds of the pastors and leaders are women. Yet, as of the present date, what he has said of the west has remained true. We in the western church continue to struggle to release our women and, in response, have battled with a dreadful state of stagnancy and compromise as well.

I believe God wants to change that, and that belief has become my passion. I will not compromise and I will not apologize. For the sake of the western church, I, like Dr. Cho, want the women released!

Vital Role

In my own life, women have truly played a vital role. My hometown was host to one seemingly solitary, yet, radical woman named *Grandma Pearl*. Grandma Pearl, as she was known by many, led countless people to the Lord. How did she do it?

One by one...

Grandma Pearl's kitchen and beauty shop became the frontlines in a war for my destiny and the destiny of many others. My mother started going to Grandma Pearl to get her hair done, but ultimately was pastored and discipled by her. Grandma Pearl eventually led my entire family to the Lord.

Later, we moved to Minnesota to work at a Christian camp led by her son and there I was called into the ministry in a dramatic Holy Spirit moment! In the middle of the Jesus People movement, my parents worked to help build up a discipleship camp for those born again on the very rough streets of Minneapolis, MN.

In the fall of 1976, my mother was on her way to a woman's meeting at our camp church. At the last minute, she asked if I wanted to go with her, which meant getting out of school and spending the day with my mother. Of course I said, "Yes." *I loved spending time with my Mama.*

Perhaps, due to my spontaneous addition to the

group that morning, we were late to the meeting and sat in the last few chairs available in the back row. I immediately found my place next to my mama on my knees using the seat of my chair as a desk and, being nine, began drawing and writing.

Completely oblivious to the meeting, I remember my mom suddenly grabbing my arm, hesitating and then finally raising me to my feet. The woman speaker at the front of the church had stopped preaching and, prompted by the Lord, was asking if there was a child in the sanctuary. Since, we were in the back row and I was sitting on the floor, she couldn't see me, but God did.

The lady preacher interrupted her sermon because the Lord had given her a prophetic message for "a child" who was at the meeting that morning. I was the only child in the congregation of about 500 women, so my mother obediently marched me down front and the woman prayed and prophesied over my life. That day was a game changer for me and a day that changed my mother's life as well, and it all came about because of Grandma Pearl.

Too OLD to Change the World?!

Quite frequently, I've had "older" women tell me that they feel they are too old to fulfill their destiny— that it has passed them by. When I ask how old they are, they often reply somewhere around 60ish. My response to them is, "Sixty is NOT old!"

At sixty, you are still a kid in God's eyes!

I often like to tell them about my mother who died when I was only sixteen years old. I only had my mother in my life for sixteen years, and yet, in that short time she laid a deep foundation in my life for an intimate relationship with Jesus.

Jesus was her best friend and she showed me through her life how He could be mine as well. She taught me so many lessons in sixteen years and, looking back, it is as if she were schooling me in Jesus and empowering me through life-lessons that have carried me through some very dark times.

So, I ask you, if you only had sixteen more years on this earth, how would you spend those sixteen years? Indeed, you can *change the world* in just sixteen years!

Never ever allow the enemy to use your age, young or old, to limit your effectiveness for the kingdom! For years, my precious grandma was a spry, young-minded woman who worked circles around people half her age, but when she hit the age of 80 I noticed something change. Her body had not changed, her mind was still sharp, but it was her thoughts that changed. She had unwittingly accepted the limitations of her age. I saw it happen, but could not convince her otherwise, she *believed* she was "old."

Grandma always had a stubborn streak and when anyone would tell her she couldn't do something, that is just what she would do. She would proudly drive eight or nine hours to visit relatives with my grandpa in tow. But, once her mindset changed to being what she considered elderly, she stopped doing that and came into agreement with the limitations of her age and she died only six years later. She's in heaven now and I know she would agree with me when I say, please don't let age limit you—we need you!

Elizabeth Ann Everest

One of my favorite historical leaders is Winston Churchill. I find his life simply fascinating. He was born into aristocracy, but felt largely unaccepted by his own parents. Overcoming the frailties of his upbringing, he lived an extraordinary life.

His life is an example of the power one person can have to affect the world. He stood as a resounding alarm and wake-up call to Britain and to the world, of the dangers of the Nazis just before WWII. He endured an onslaught of public animosity from a people who were beleaguered by WWI and did not want to accept the fact that another war would so soon be upon them.

Though, at the time, no one wanted to hear what Churchill had to say, he refused to let it stop him. He continued to sound the alarm until people realized the danger they were in.

I believe his life can stand as a prophetic example to us as to the power of our own voice. Whether you are a woman or a man, you can stand in the gap for the world. The power of one life passionately driven to be the voice of hope and victory can, indeed, liberate thousands from tyranny.

After laboring almost alone during the beginning years of WWII, Britain was, perhaps, relieved when Japan attacked America, because they knew that, at last, their American allies would enter the war and help them. Traveling to America to encourage our nation, he gave a great speech to the U.S. Congress on December 26, 1941.

During this memorable occasion, his American audience welcomed him with thunderous applause.

Before, treated with disdain, no one wanted to listen to Churchill because his message, although true, was not the message people *wanted to hear*. But he was, unfortunately, proven right and suddenly thousands gladly, even tearfully, listened to his every word.

In the moment selected for him by God's design, he spoke. "Sure I am this day—now we are the masters of our fate; that the task which has been set us is not above our strength; that its pangs and toils are not beyond our endurance. As long as we have faith in our cause and an unconquerable will-power, salvation will not be denied us. In the words of the Psalmist, 'He shall not be afraid of evil tidings; his heart is fixed, trusting in the Lord.' Not all the tidings will be evil."[2]

Many historians who've written of Churchill's life give credit for his amazing tenacity and strength to one woman, *Elizabeth Ann Everest*, his nanny. It was Elizabeth who gave Churchill the keys of a faith in God that enabled him to change the world. So, in heavens' history it will be recorded that Elizabeth Ann Everest, nanny, did, indeed, change the world and save not only Britain, but all the allied forces.

Elizabeth was a 43 year old woman when she was employed by the Churchill family and remained in their service for 18 years. What she did in those 18 years simply astounded the heavens!

(1) http://www.charismamag.com/life/women/1832
8-what-dr-cho-taught-me-about-women-in-revival

(2) http://ghostsofdc.org/2012/03/14/the-masters-
of-our-fate-winston-churchill-addresses-congress-
1942/

8

It Will Not Be
Taken From Her

"There is only one thing worth being concerned about.
Mary has discovered it, and it will not be taken away from
her" Luke 10:42 NLT.

DOCTRINAL ANTAGONISTS have tried for
centuries to make unequal distinctions between men
and women. Yet, it was God, Himself, who made us
equal and bound us together. It is together, as men
and women, that we are the strongest. The enemy
knows that fact to be true. That is why he's used
human weakness and pride through history to exploit
us by imposing a premise of preeminence between
the genders. It's his attempt to redefine the very
fundamental origins of mankind. The end result, he
hopes, will destroy our souls.

In an attempt to separate and divide mankind,
the divisions between the sexes are demonic and
directly opposed to God's divine plan for humanity.
Truly, we are all in desperate need of the grace of
God, but He gives His grace to the humble. It is pride
which seeks to make distinctions between people of
different races, gender and social standing to puff us
up and rob us of our portion of our Father's great
grace.

Sexism is a trap set for our humanity, like racism and any measure of hatred, a trap meant for the destruction of our soul. For, "The Lord detests double standards of every kind..." (Proverbs 20:10 NLT emphasis mine).

Throughout history, many have wrestled with the Scriptures in an effort to strengthen the divide between the genders, continuing this divisive teaching. They believed that God simply referring to Himself as our Father somehow indicates His masculine nature and, therefore, proves men are superior. Yet, Genesis 1:27 states women were made in His likeness. But in addition to that, God (our Father) refers to Himself as a mother as well.

In Job 38:29, God refers to His womb. In Isaiah 42:14, the servant of the Lord refers to God as a woman in labor. And in Isaiah 46:3-4, He refers to Him as a pregnant woman. But the most compelling scripture about God our "mother" is Isaiah 66:13. The Lord says, "As a mother comforts her child, so will I comfort you; and you will be comforted over Jerusalem" (NIV). Am I saying that God is a woman? No. He is Spirit, but has both masculine and feminine characteristics.

As a first year student in a well-known Bible college in the USA, my oldest daughter, Cassandra, found herself the focal point of a debate in which she was being asked to prove men and women were both made in God's image. Showing them the Scriptural passages referencing our design in Genesis, they were silent.

Astonished and in disbelief, the men refused to continue the debate with her. As she showed them the truth in Scripture, they refused to believe it because they had been taught tradition and not the reality of God's intended design. And they had, "...let go of the commands of God and [were] holding on to human traditions" (Mark 7:8 NIV emphasis mine).

It's so sad that both men and women want so badly to find some reason to exclude women from representing God. Yet, God is not male or female in the physical, but He is Spirit. The church has traditionally taught that since God is male, only men can truly represent Him. Unfortunately, it's given them a sense of superiority. But is that what they really want?

Although they may argue the point of their superiority vehemently, what do they get out of it? Just the fleeting feeling of a favorable position—that's all. Yet, all the while God is drawing nearer and nearer to the humble, to those they attack with their discrimination. If our hearts are pure and we are truly seeking to know God, we should be looking for ways to humble ourselves, running away from anything that would cause us to puff ourselves up.

It's important that men stand up and fight for the equality of women, for their soul as well as for women. And some are. Yet, often it is men who fight against the equality and release of women. By accepting even a small distinction between the genders, they are making themselves superior to women and, in essence, fighting against the plans of God being manifested in the lives of countless generations of women.

As husbands, fathers and brothers, men can be mighty warriors fighting against the enemy's war on women (Genesis 3:15), fighting as if their souls depended upon it, because they do. Indeed, none of us want to find ourselves on the side against God. Fighting for our Father's kingdom, we must determine not to hand down a morsel of traditional disdain to our daughters.

Gentlemen, stand and declare with us, "Not my daughters! Truly! My children, and especially my daughters, will know who they are in Christ and not be limited by the error of mankind. For, my daughter is His daughter!"

The Controversial Women Issue

When my family and I moved to the south we checked out different local churches. Searching through their websites, I was in disbelief at what I found. Again and again, I found on public websites in "Bylaws" or "About Us" or "What We Believe," in many different ways they said the same thing, "We don't believe in women!" They listed the women issue under the category of "Controversial Issues" and stated how they stood on it. Many stated that they took what they believed was a moderate stance on the issue of women, ie. complementarianism.

Truly, complementarianism, the belief that the roles of men and women in marriage, family life and religious leadership are different, but complement each other, is not truth. It's a compromised truth that leaves way too much room for confusion and abuse. Truly, there is no such thing as compromised truth. Indeed, it is still a lie.

Abuse and bias is not moderate to the one being abused and rejected. Simply by limiting women at all sends a clear message: We don't' approve of you! You're not good enough! You're not what you need to be! God doesn't love you as much as men! You are unacceptable! You're stupid! You're second class!

Here's my least favorite: you're not as human as a man. That's crazy! And, yet, more than half of church attendees are women. Why is it okay to send such a derogatory message to women?

If we were referring to black people that way, the NAACP would be at our door with a hefty lawsuit! So, why is it okay to treat women as if they are second-class citizens when the Word of God says clearly there is no more "male and female" (Galatians 3:28)? We cannot be sympathetic to anything that will limit our daughters, the church or the harvest.

What I've discovered is: in today's world, men are not the only perpetrators of sexism. No. Sexism in the church is ALSO propagated by women who do not know the truth. They've been so used to the lies told to them for countless centuries, they believe it's not Christlike to be what God designed them to be and they hold tight to the traditions of generations.

By our responses to wrongful treatment, we teach others how to treat us. Truly, what we tolerate will become the standard of how we are treated in the future. But, if we do not know how we should be treated or what is proper civility, how can we teach others what is expected?

Our traditional family values are only good if they line up with what Jesus taught us. If they become a bondage and a snare, they are working for the enemy and not us. In Luke 8:21, Jesus redefines who the family unit is.

"Now Jesus' mother and brothers came to see him, but they were not able to get near him because of the crowd. Someone told him, 'Your mother and brothers are standing outside, wanting to see you.' He replied, 'My mother and brothers are those who hear God's word and put it into practice.'" Luke 8:19-21 NIV.

First and foremost, we are all His children if we follow His leading and we are just as human and just as loved by the Father. We are just as capable of representing Christ. Indeed, the only qualification for the family of God is Luke 8:21. Isn't that marvelous?

Oppressive Expectations

Years ago, as I visited with a friend of mine who struggled in her marriage because she felt her husband did not exemplify the leadership qualities of the traditional "man of the house." She felt vulnerable and frustrated, because she believed her husband was not living up to the ideals of the Christian community. These ideals implied that men have some kind of divine or magical leadership power. Wow! Truly, that's a lot of pressure to put on someone, isn't it? Men and women were made in God's image, but neither are divine or all-powerful.

I told my friend, "The leader of the family is the one who leads and others follow them." That's all it is. If people follow you, you are a leader. My friend was just that. Her children and even her husband followed her. She wasn't bossy. She was a confident, wise and humble leader that people just naturally followed. Her husband did not possess the same leadership qualities, but he did possess other qualities of equal value to his family.

Why do we put so much pressure on ourselves and others to fit into the "ideal" mold of what families should look and act like? God designed us all uniquely and His creation of the family is just as unique. Every individual family is created differently, because God is creative and enjoys variety.

I hate it when I hear men (or women) refer to the "good ol' days" and they say, "Back when men were men..." What an atrocious thing to say! You've just condemned every man who doesn't line up with what your opinion of men should be, as if to say that rough and tough, macho men are the definition of masculinity and anything less is unacceptable or wrong. No, a real man is God's creation, not yours.

When people stop defining what other people should be or become, the happier we will be as a society. Let them be who God has made them to be. Your opinions are just that—your opinions. And opinions are of little value, as they change constantly.

My family and I are friends with another family in which the father of that family loves to cook, clean, decorate and organize, attributes stereotypically assigned to females. If you are ever privileged enough to sample his cooking, you will be blessed indeed! When he cooks, you taste the anointing in his food and while he cooks you can see his God-given giftings at work. His wife could feel insecure that she does not have the giftings her husband has, but she doesn't. She has found her security in Jesus. She, more than anyone, compliments her husband and is his best advertisement! It works for them because it is led by the Spirit of God. How frustrating for both of them if they were told they had to switch roles because they don't line up with gender stereotypes.

Mary or Martha

The Lord spoke to me years ago, "Victoria, you can be a Mary or a Martha, but you can't be both." It took me years before I really understood what He meant by that.

Mary and Martha were two sisters who followed Jesus and were discipled by Him. Jesus was obviously very good friends with both sisters, but Mary seemed to respond to the importance of what He was teaching by giving up all other seemingly important activities to learn at His feet. Martha, her sister, reacted differently. She felt that preparing His meal was more important and was upset by Mary's refusal to help her prepare it. Their struggle created an opportunity for Jesus to give them both instruction on what He truly desired from them.

Mary embraced all that Jesus wanted to give her. She put Jesus and the relationship He offered her ahead of the expectations of society. But Martha, her sister, did not. Indeed, Martha thought Jesus expected her to maintain her role as the dutiful, ideal Jewish woman. Not only did she feel strongly about her opinion of the proper role of women in the home, but she demanded that Jesus scold Mary for not doing it with her. He refused (Luke 10:38-40).

"'Martha, Martha,' the Lord answered, 'you are worried and upset about many things, but few things are needed—or indeed only one. Mary has chosen what is better, and it will not be taken away from her'" (Luke 10:41-42 NIV).

What?! Did Jesus just say it was more important to sit at His feet and learn from Him than fulfill the traditional role of a woman? Surely, He misunderstood the rules! No, He was very clear; Mary had chosen to become His disciple—it was her choice. Jesus protected Mary's right to choose!

Women have a choice in how they live their lives. We were created for God's pleasure and it gives Him great pleasure to see us walking with Him through this life, enjoying the giftings He's given us. As women, we represent Him well as we follow the leading of His Spirit.

Honestly, I enjoy housework, but it does not define who I am. It is just something I enjoy, like long walks, devouring history and the Word of God. When God told me I could choose either to be Mary or Martha, He was developing in me the recognition of my right to choose and not letting the ideas and ideologies of others dictate my life. He affirmed to me that it was my choice. I could try and measure up to society's idea of what I'm worth OR I could just enjoy Him and become all He's created me to be.

He wants you to choose! Will you follow Him or mankind? So I say to you, sisters and brothers: You can be Mary or you can be Martha, but you can't be both!

Blessed Rather

Like me, Jesus amazed another woman in Luke 11:27-28. She received a compelling challenge from Him when she chose to define her worth through the lives of the children she bore, which was traditionally the gauge of a woman's value in society.

A woman in the crowd called out to Jesus, "Blessed is the mother who gave you birth and nursed you" (vs. 27 NIV). But, He answered back, "Blessed rather are those who hear the word of God and obey it" (vs. 28 NIV).

Jesus was, indeed, revolutionizing the way women thought about their lives. Christ challenged women to reconsider who they were and what they were created for.

Surely, Jesus did not think it was a bad thing to be grateful for the children they had been blessed with when he spoke to the woman the way He did. But His response indicates there was more going on with her comment than what we can read simply. He answered her and said, "Blessed rather are those who hear the word of God and obey it."

Again, Jesus tried to redefine her worth and give her a choice. Women at that time were told their only value was in having babies, and so women naturally defined their worth by their children. So many women do that still today. That is what Jesus was trying to get her to correct in her vision of herself. He wanted her to value herself, not by her role as a mother or by the greatness of her children, but by living for Him.

Do Not Grieve the Spirit

Women have been in ministry throughout the centuries to whatever degree they were allowed at the time. Especially during times of revival when the Spirit was poured out, women were used to a much greater degree. But, when the revival died down, they were relocated back to the nursery, kitchen and Sunday school classes.

Historically, we have had to ask ourselves, what contributed to the diminishing effects of the Spirit's presence in revival? Was it our insensitive reinstatement of our own ideological, man-made traditional roles in church OR was it the hurtful process of demoting women that grieved Holy Spirit and ended the revivals?

If, in revival, God's Spirit is manifested and subsequently erases the lines of gender and race, how is it we do not understand that those lines are offensive to our Father? When the Spirit comes, He establishes the order according to heaven's standards. Who are we then to change them back to mankind's standards?

Women were designed to bless God in whatever capacity He calls them to. So, truly, the war between the sexes is really a war between heaven and earth. Ask yourself, who would you like to see win this war?

In Scripture, we find women apostles, prophets, teachers, writers, warriors and even a judge. If God ordained women as spiritual leaders in the old testament with the old covenant, how much more would He be pleased by them now ministering within the established new covenant?

No Apologies

I've heard so many women in ministry say things like, "A man was given my anointing first, but he didn't want it, so it fell to me"—that just doesn't make sense! If God wanted a male to have your anointing, He could surely find another man who would take it. God wanted to give the anointing and calling to you because you were His first choice.

Never apologize for your calling. That's like calling God foolish. Of course He knew you were a woman when He called you, and for that reason you are perfect for the anointing He has for you!

As women, I think we tend to apologize for our giftings and callings because we feel the pressure of a society that has yet to embrace the kingdom of heaven's value system. So, we excuse our ministry, apologizing for our gender. Human nature is just crafty and jealous—men and women alike.

As women who represent our Father God, we have to ask ourselves a question: will we bow to the world or to our God? Will we fear more the chastisement of those who feel women should remain what history has claimed them to be, or become what heaven would like us to become?

The Word of God in Luke 11:36 says, "Therefore, if your whole body is full of light, and no part of it dark, it will be just as full of light as when a lamp shines its light on you" (NIV). The body of Christ will not shine with the true light of heaven until we are whole and every part of us is lit up and brightly shining as one.

Biblical Rule or Traditional Rule

In church years ago, I taught a prophetic class. I asked my husband to join with me in the group, but I was the teacher and leader of the group. Because my husband was involved in it with me, the church staff kept putting his name before mine in the information packet. I honestly didn't care, but my husband was very bothered by it and went to them repeatedly to have them change it and put my name first.

Steve has fought these gender bias battles alongside me, and he gets offended when he sees others trying to impose those stereotypes on him. He does truly get offended when, just because he's the man, people try to hand him the mic and "promote" him ahead of me. It really does bother him, because he understands the meaning and purpose behind it. And he doesn't agree.

When my husband and I started my ministry, I again asked him to be a part of it publicly with me, but he declined. He said, "If my name is involved, people will automatically demote you and make me the focus. I won't have it!"

Over the years, many women have contacted me and asked my opinion regarding their need for a male covering over their ministry. Of course my first reaction is that they already have one in the Lord Jesus Christ. Truly, this teaching is destructive and demonic—it makes me very upset, because, besides being stupid (and unscriptural), it has ruined so many fruitful ministries.

Frequently, women have banded together to pray or teach and the Holy Spirit has powerfully anointed their meetings with growing numbers of women attending. Then someone comes along and tells them they're not doing it right! Imposing their own opinion, they demand they have a male covering before their ministry can continue. Dutifully, the women stop, but find no man willing to cover them. So, the ministry ends.

Why do women find it so difficult to accept their equality? Why do they fight against the blessings and freedoms Christ died to give them? Why do we knock each other down, instead of lifting each other to freedom in our calling?

As a woman, there are many beliefs in the church

that I would be willing to put up with. But when I see the negative effects on my daughters and how they are effected by the beliefs I accept, I can no longer just put up with things as they are. I must speak out. All these little idiosyncrasies take a toll on relationships, and for what? Just a traditional point of view.

If we hold on to the traditions of man, we are giving our children an inheritance of lies. We are eroding their strength before they can learn to stand and our sons are handed a load too heavy to bear— one they were not created to handle on their own. The burdens of the family were meant to be shared by two, not one. It is too much for one person, we need each other.

If we follow the leading of the Holy Spirit and embrace the truth in God's Word, we stand together, united in the strength derived from one another.

9

Revolution

"You have let go of the commands of God and are holding on to human traditions" Genesis 1:27 NIV.

SEVERAL YEARS AGO, my youngest daughter, CailieEllen, was in our church's Christmas music program. As the musical opened, it was a delightful presentation of the Christmas story, except for the beginning when they enacted a "humorous" rendition of the fall of creation.

In the play, Eve was alone with the serpent. She, along with the snake, schemed together to deceive Adam with stolen fruit. The audience roared with laughter as the scene progressed, but I was in shock. I was taken aback as I remembered the months of practice CailieEllen had put in for the performance. All I could think was, "My little girl has been watching this very twisted version of creation acted out for months!"

It is honestly astonishing to me how many people believe that rendition of the creation story, but it's not Biblical, nor is it even logical. If people would study the Scriptures, they would know the Word says Eve was not alone when the serpent bombarded the couple with his lies.

Quite the contrary, it says, "The woman was convinced. She saw that the tree was beautiful and its fruit looked delicious, and she wanted the wisdom it would give her. So she took some of the fruit and ate it. Then she gave some to her husband, **who was with her**, and he ate it, too" Genesis 3:6 NLT (emphasis mine). Some versions of Scripture leave that part out.

The rendering of that small portion of Scripture clearly contradicts the belief Eve was alone with the serpent when mankind fell into sin. Through the omission of that part of scripture we also see what is obvious: through the centuries as the Scriptures have been translated and re-translated, there has been, unfortunately, a bias against women.

Shared Tragedy vs. Greek Myth!

To truly unravel the evolution of a lie, we have to ask, "Where did this destructive thinking originate?"

The premise that Eve was alone with the serpent when she ate the fruit and Adam ate it unknowingly is not scriptural. But that belief was actually adopted from Greek mythology, not the Word of God.

In actuality, the tragedy of the fall is shared by both Adam and Eve. The word "you" in Hebrew has two meanings. It can mean you as in a single person, or plural. The word used in this case has the plural meaning.

So, Satan was talking to more than one person, saying, "[Y'all (a nod to my Texas friends)] will not certainly die," the serpent said to the woman. "For God knows that when you eat from it your eyes will be opened, and you will be like God, knowing good and evil" Genesis 3:4-5 NIV.

And when Eve answered the serpent, in Genesis 3:2, she says, "we," answering for them both.

The Marginalization of God's Gift

It's no secret that the Greek society, although beautiful in some aspects, was notorious for their perversion. Seeking to justify their deviant treatment of women and depraved ideology, the Greeks transformed the lineage of women. Through diabolical lies now considered philosophical or scientific by many, women were relegated to soul-less creatures, created for reproduction and sexual pleasure.

Even in society today, the Greeks are still quite infamous for their degradation. Much like our modern media is used to sculpt the beliefs of our society, the ancient Greeks used their dramas, poetry and speeches to infuse their culture with a disparaging view of women.

Through their mythology, they maligned Eve, comparing her to Pandora, a fictional character, who alone, opened the door to the release of sin and the fall of mankind, essentially blaming her for all the evils of the world. Sadly, the permeating lies took hold and as the influence of the Greek society was so pervasive, and adopted by the Romans, God's gift was successfully maligned.

History reveals men believed women to be more easily tempted by evil and therefore needed to be dominated by men. They believed that a woman must be legally under the control of either their father or brother until they were married. Then, of course, their husband took possession of them. As difficult as married life may have been for them, it was far worse to be single. Many young single women in Greek society were used as prostitutes to raise money for the government.

Also, it was believed women were inferior in intelligence. Honestly, I can't blame men for thinking that, in as much as women throughout history, and even now, hide their intelligence in an effort to attract men. Truly, the misguided thought being, men would never want a woman with brains, is such a pity. The Greeks wanted to believe women were ineducable, so they could disregard their humanity.

Regrettably, many Jewish leaders picked up on the dehumanizing, disparaging Greco-Roman lies against women and incorporated them into their literature addressed to Jewish society. Thus began the marginalization of women. Rabbis like Philo of Alexandria seemed to thrive on the degrading teachings of the Greco-Roman society and found ways to adopt them into Jewish writings. With obvious bias against women, these men imposed their attitudes in the Talmud and Mishmah in an effort to control and dominate. The rules against women were so harsh, it essentially reveals their *fear* of women.

In a shoddy attempt to disguise their contempt for women in the guise of pious religious consideration, women were systematically reduced to, at best, second-class citizens and usually much worse. It was taught that women were to blame for any lustful feelings generated in men. In response, the religiously pious men would go to great lengths to completely ignore women, and therefore began the belief that the more you ignored or abhorred women, the more pious you were seen to be. Soon, it became illegal for a man to even speak to a woman he wasn't related to.

Jewish Teachings Against Women

Much like the lies to destroy the humanity of the Jewish race preceding the holocaust during WWII, the enemy bombarded mankind with lies against women and inhuman laws were set into place to *guard* the civility of men against the so-called "depravity of women."

One such teaching was expressed, "A woman is inferior to her husband in all things. Let her, therefore, be obedient to him" (Apion 2:25). *Flavius Josephus

It also taught that "Let the words of the law be burned rather than committed to women... If a man teaches his daughter the law, it is as though he taught her lewdness." (Sotah 3:4) *Talmud.

Another charge stated, "Let a curse come upon the man who must needs have his wife or children say grace for him." (4) *Talmud. Can you just imagine?

And yet another heinous belief from their reprehensible teachings, "It is well for those whose children are male, but ill for those whose children are female... At the birth of a boy all are joyful, but at the birth of a girl all are sad... When a boy comes into the world, peace comes into the world; when a girl comes, nothing comes...Even *the most virtuous of women is a witch*" (Niddah 31b) *Tohorat.

In Jewish teachings, you can see how far women had fallen since God gifted them to mankind, and all of this accumulated just before God brought forth His promised redemption through the *seed of the woman* (Genesis 3:15) to annihilate the *fallen condition* of mankind with the salvation of Jesus Christ. Indeed, Jesus liberated women and He deserves the credit for saving women from the unjust derision of the depravity of human nature. It is He who started the restoration of women, and expected His followers to advance it. Some did...

A Bondage Breaker

One of the Scriptures often used to attack my daughter, Cassandra, was 1 Corinthians 14:34-35, "Women should be silent during the church meetings. It is not proper for them to speak. They should be submissive just as the law says. If they have any questions, they should ask their husbands at home, for it is improper for women to speak in church meetings" (emphasis mine).

It wasn't enough for me to give Cassandra my interpretation of this scripture, for it was a weapon launched against her—a bomb that would go off whenever the enemy wanted to destroy her peace. I had to defuse it! So, we have to remind ourselves that 1 and 2 Corinthians were written by Paul to the Christians in Corinth to address the *specific issues they were having.*

In chapter 14, Paul addressed their problems with prophesy in their meetings. The entire chapter is devoted to addressing proper use of tongues and prophesy, except for verses 34-35, which seem to suddenly switch to addressing women speaking in church meetings.

If you will understand the social climate of their day, you have to know that up until this time, women were not even allowed to know much about the

Torah (Bible), and with only a few exceptions, they were not allowed to prophesy. The Jewish rabbis taught that it was a degradation for a man, husband, father or brother to teach their female relatives anything about God.

With Christ's new way of love, the women were suddenly included in what they were formerly excluded from. Of course, it was all brand new to the Corinthian believers, so their church services got a little chaotic. Historically, until the time of Pentecost, prophesy was not for everyone, and usually only the "super-spiritual" people prophesied. So, they were simply unfamiliar with how to go about using the gifts.

Truly, the chaos they experienced is better than bondage. They eventually learned how to use the gifts in an orderly manner to become a true blessing to the church.

Paul's teaching at this time was "in your face" revolutionary and went against the teachings of the Jewish rabbis. He taught that the common man could prophesy and, also, women were liberated. He constantly taught against the ideology that women could not be taught about God. Paul insisted they must be taught about God saying, "if they want to inquire about something, they should ask their own husbands at home" (1 Corinthians 14:35) and not disrupt the service. He thought it was a shame and was disgusted by the fact that women were kept from the knowledge of their God and ostracized in the temple. So, he instructs husbands, who had previously been taught the Scriptures, to teach their wives.

Paul stood as an aggressive *bondage-breaker* for women.

In fact, he, more than any other disciple, stood for liberty for women. He taught men to honor women, like he asked in Romans 16:1-2, "I commend to you our sister Phoebe, a deacon of the church in Cenchreae. I ask you to receive her in the Lord in a way worthy of his people and to give her any help she may need from you, for she has been the benefactor of many people, including me" (NIV). Paul presented Pheobe to the church as a deacon, elder and servant of Christ, using the same words he used when he referenced himself and Timothy (Philippians 1:1) and when he described the qualifications of deacons, elders and servants (1Timothy 3:8-12).

So, if, in his letter to the Corinthians, he is supposedly making a blanket statement suddenly saying women can't speak in church, then we have to ask ourselves, "Was Paul mentally ill?" Because this would be a huge departure from his entreating for Christians to honor Phoebe, a woman elder in the church in Cenchreae.

Even more remarkable, Paul also commended Junia, a woman apostle, who was held in prison for preaching the Gospel at the same time Paul was. Of her he said, "Salute Andronicus and Junia, my kinsmen, and my fellow prisoners, *who are of note among the apostles*, who also were in Christ before me" (Romans 16:7 KJV).

Paul also supported Lydia and Chloe, who lead home-churches or local flocks (Acts 16:40, 1 Corinthians 1:11).

However, I believe the most notable female influence on Paul's life was Priscilla, who discipled him in the faith and of whom he spoke of as being equal to himself (Romans 16:3). If He is now saying women shouldn't speak in church, he seems to have suddenly changed his mind, if that's the case. But it simply is not.

In light of Paul's previous assistance to female ministers, we have to take a deeper look at 1 Corinthians 14:34-35. You have to understand the unbridled excitement that filled those in attendance at the Corinthian's meetings; you can see how it could easily turn chaotic. For, until this time, the women knew very little of scriptures and as people were prophesying, they wanted to know more about everything that was being said. So, as Paul writes to them, he stops in mid-stream during his talk about the use of the gifts and simply states that if women want to know more about prophesy, wait until after service to ask their husbands at home so as not to interrupt the flow of the meetings. Because his letter's objective was *orderly services* that were more productive.

Women were singled out because their husbands had previously been receiving teaching from the Word and women had not, so they were using time in the service to ask questions. Paul again was imploring husbands to teach their wives because he wanted women to have an understanding of the Scriptures.

He wasn't saying women couldn't prophesy, no. He was saying to let them ask questions about it at home and not to disrupt the flow of the services with questions that could be answered at home by their husbands who were already privy to Biblical training. Remember, Paul was constantly referring to men and women as he encouraged them both to prophesy, etc. So, he wasn't saying they couldn't talk. Obviously, you have to talk to prophesy.

Revolutionary

Paul's teaching about the equality of the sexes was unparalleled in the early church. He taught that a wife had equal rights and access to her husband's body. That was a huge deal, courageous and was in direct contrast to the beliefs of the day, which stated that a wife had absolutely no rights whatsoever over her own body or her husband's.

So, when he stated that "The wife does not have authority over her own body, but yields it to her husband. In the same way, the husband does not have authority over his own body, but yields it to his wife" (1 Corinthians 7:4 NIV), he was contradicting Jewish teachings. That's why he said women should submit, but he also taught that men should submit to women as well in Ephesians 5:21, "Submit to one another out of reverence for Christ" (NIV).

Paul was a courageous revolutionary and his teaching brought liberty to women, not bondage!

It doesn't make sense that he would teach anything else. He was leading the church in a revolution and it was up to him to bring order to the revolution as much as he could. It's unconscionable that those same scriptures are now used to destroy and divide men and women.

Much like the Israelites who were held in captivity for 400 years and then suddenly released, as women, we have to realize who we really are. Truly, who we've always been, but didn't know it. We cannot continue to cling to a slave mentality, like the nation of Israel after it had gained freedom. Like a slave nation, ineligible of equal citizenship, women also have been beat down by the negative treatment they have endured for centuries.

Many women believe it is more spiritual to think of themselves as lowly and incapable and, in turn, expect divine behavior from their very human husbands. Truly, they don't understand who God created them to be!

As a church, we need to patiently and prayerfully encourage women to walk in the spiritual and societal freedom Christ died to give them. We, as a church, will not be made whole until we fight for all of us to live in the knowledge of who we are in Christ. For, we are ALL one in Christ!

IO

The Way Of Love

"Therefore be imitators of God, as beloved children; and
walk in love, just as Christ also loved you and gave
Himself up for us, an offering and a sacrifice to God as a
fragrant aroma" Ephesians 5:1-2 NIV.

WHEN I WAS a young woman, I thought Paul the
apostle was dreadfully sexist and the things I
understood him to teach about women did not line
up with what Jesus taught or what Father God told
me about myself. So, for years I just really didn't give
too much attention to Paul's teachings on women. I
chose to follow the leading of the Spirit and looked to
the rest of the Bible and its view on women.

It wasn't until years later when my daughter,
Cassandra, was being abused by Christian misogynists
who used Paul's teachings to strip her of the intimate
friendship she had developed with her heavenly
Father that I was forced then to take a deeper look at
what Paul was really saying. These derisive "voices of
destruction" had used Scripture to devour my
daughter's destiny and convince her God did not love
her. So, naturally, as her mom, I labored to fight
against their contemptuous theology and save her.

I knew I could not just talk her out of what these
people had convinced her of with my own thoughts

and beliefs, because Cassandra has never been the type of person who is easily convinced about anything until it has been proven. No, they had used the Word to destroy her, so I would have to find the evidence in the Word to prove to her that God valued her as much as He valued any man.

The power of the lies that assaulted her heart forced me to study hard and dig deep for Cassandra and all the women like her who had been told God made them to be second-class humans. As I sought after the heart of my Father to save her, the Holy Spirit opened my eyes to the truth of who Paul was and what he was actually trying to achieve with his teachings.

In order to truly understand Paul's writings, we have to first understand that, although spiritually rich, his teachings were not written to be a part of the Bible. He did not even write them with the thought they would become a book. They were simply letters, for the most part, written to specific groups of Christians. Paul sought to bring revelation and guidance to specific areas of their beliefs and church actions through his letters.

In understanding the culture and the particular trials of these individual churches, we have a much better idea of what Paul was trying to say to them and why. Without that, we end up with misconstrued theories of what Paul believed and his teachings become a misguided tool to destroy what he was trying to liberate and protect (Galatians 3:1-21).

If you line up and analyze *everything* Paul said about women, you may start to get the idea that he suffered from dissociative identity disorder or was just plain nuts. One day he said one thing and the next day it sounds like he's saying the exact opposite. Depending on what you want to teach or impose as theology, you can take your pick and twist what he's said to match your beliefs. But in doing that, you do not have truth and truth is what the Word of God is all about.

God's Word, including Paul's letters, are for guidance and teaching us to walk in a new manner of thinking—a new way of viewing ourselves and relating to the people we are in relationship with. The Word of God is our map and guide to experience *the joys of community* and essentially releasing the kingdom of heaven on earth (John 15:10-11).

Spirit-guided Relationships

Included in the Bible are letters Paul wrote to the Christians in the cities of Rome, Ephesus, Colossi, Corinth, Galatia, Thessalonica and Philippi. He had previously taught the believers in these cities and followed up with letters to guide them in their faith—to strengthen their development in the new way of relating to one another that he had previously introduced to them.

In the natural worldly-way of thinking, there is a hierarchy of sorts: master over slave, parent over child and husband over wife—this is the natural consequence of sin and selfishness. Unfortunately, many people who have authority will be corrupted by it, but that is not God's way. In His kingdom, those who have authority are accountable to God for how they use the authority given to them.

Our Lord taught in Mark 10:42-44 that manifestation of spiritual authority is quite different than natural or worldly authority. He said, "You know that those who are regarded as rulers of the Gentiles lord it over them, and their high officials exercise authority over them. Not so with you. Instead, whoever wants to become great among you must be your servant, and whoever wants to be first must be slave of all" (NIV).

In Ephesians 5:21-30, Paul endeavored to reinforce this new way of living by focusing on three different inter-relational groups of people: husbands and wives, parents and children, and masters and slaves. He first addresses the marriage relationship and says, we must "submit to one another out of reverence for Christ," then adds, "For wives, this means submit to your husbands as to the Lord" and "husbands, this means love your wives, just as Christ loved the church." The church has put far too much emphasis on the words, *submit* and *love* and not enough on the *how*. I believe, Paul's goal was to accent the *as to the Lord* and *as Christ loved the church* parts of the Scripture. His goal was to institute Christ's actions in marriage, and because of Christ we submit to *one another* first and foremost!

In Ephesians 6:1-4 he addresses the relationship between parent and child and saying, "Children, obey your parents because you belong to the Lord" and "Fathers (and mothers) do not provoke your children to anger by the way you treat them. And then in Ephesians 6:5-9 he says, "Slaves, obey your earthly masters with deep respect and fear. Serve them as you would serve Christ" and "Masters, treat your slaves in the same way. Don't threaten them; remember, you both have the same Master in heaven, and he has no favorites."

Although they are not equal in accordance to man's fallen nature, through the cross we can begin to live as our Father intended we should, living as eternal beings, equal in His kingdom on Earth. Christ came to restore our true identity to us which is the Father's reality. And as we live in accordance to heaven's kingdom, we manifest heaven's reality in this life. Therefore, His kingdom comes to earth, His will is done on earth and we become a portal for heaven to manifest on earth.

It is so incredibly unfortunate that the church has emphasized worldly submission rather than the liberty of the Spirit. The church should be the first to champion for equality. But sadly, many have focused on teaching submission to those deemed as subservient by a fallen world and placed heavy burdens on them that they themselves would never want to carry. In essence, they force them to live in accordance to their fallen nature and not as the new creations Christ intended. Truly, this is the exact opposite of what Paul was trying to do. That's the thinking of the natural world—the fallen world. Like Christ, Paul was a revolutionary!

Culturally, it was simply unheard of to insist on equal status to those people the world deemed subservient. The eternal value of the women in Paul's time was not deemed relevant; their humanity had been compromised by society as they had little more value than livestock. Men were never taught to consider their wives as anything more than another possession they "owned."

Yet, Paul revolutionized relationships by simply stating that they were equal in Christ. "There is neither Jew nor Gentile, neither slave nor free, nor is there male and female, for you are all one in Christ Jesus" (Galatians 3:28 NIV).

In the natural, masters, parents and husbands owned their slaves, children and wives, and as they were considered legal property, it was lawful for them to be treated grievously, even killing them in some instances. They were literally dehumanized by humanity and Paul was shattering the narrow-minded thinking of his generation. With his courage and audacity, he not only said it was okay, but it was their duty to treat others as they themselves would want to be treated. In saying as much, he regarded them as their equals, worthy of equal respect.

God loves the humanity He created, and any action that dehumanizes another individual is not from Him. God sent His Son to die for humanity; He did not send Jesus to kill, dehumanize or dominate it.

It was the Father's plan to give us life and salvation. He fought for humanity, to raise up the brokenhearted and strengthen those cast down by society. He sent Jesus to liberate those held in bondage by control, beaten down and dominated.

"The Spirit of the Sovereign LORD is upon me, for the LORD has anointed me to bring good news to the poor. He has sent me to comfort the brokenhearted and *to proclaim that captives will be released and prisoners will be freed"* Isaiah 61:1 NLT (emphasis mine).

The Way of Love

To the churches mentioned above, Paul wrote to show them the way of Christ, which is *the way of love.* In teaching them how to behave toward each other, he was helping them represent Christ to unbelievers in society. He said, "Be very careful, then, how you live—not as unwise but as wise, making the most of every opportunity, because the days are evil" (Ephesians 5:15-16 NIV).

He wanted the Christian household to be an example to the world of how we should live and treat each other with mutual respect and love, *submitting to one another out of their love and reverence for Christ* (Ephesians 5:21). In Christ, we should be competing to out-submit each other! Our challenge should be: who can honor more—who can esteem more—or who can appreciate and bless others the most!

Paul went so far as to tell the men to *love their wives as Christ loved the church* (Ephesians 5:25) and he blew them away when he told them to love their wives as themselves and to treat them as they would treat themselves. "After all, no one ever hated their own body, but they feed and care for their body, just as Christ does the church—for we are members of his body" Ephesians 5:29-30 NIV.

This powerful revelation had never been taught before. It was likely offensive to their way of thinking. It was difficult for them to humble themselves and treat their wives as equals when they had been taught so wrongly for so long. The way of love was simply revolutionary!

Mutual Respect

The way of love was the way of *mutual respect* and esteem. The way of love did away with the ideas of inequality, giving equivalent authority to those who'd previously been deemed subservient. It suddenly created a platform for them to display the love of Christ to each other in their own home as an example to the world.

Paul taught the children to obey their parents, because this was the right and honorable thing to do before the Lord (Ephesians 6:1-3). But, in turn, he told parents not to exasperate their children and cause them to become bitter or angry, "instead, bring them up in the training and instruction of the Lord" (Ephesians 6:4 NIV).

The *instruction of the Lord* he is referencing is *the way of the love* he was teaching them. He wanted to make sure this revolutionary teaching took hold of society and was passed on to each generation—transforming the world!

Yes, he told slaves to obey their earthly masters with sincerity of heart, and to work for them as though they were working for the Lord. But he told them this so that by their example they would win their masters to Christ.

The way of love was a way for the Christians to show the world how different they were—to give the world hope. Christ had told them, "A new command I give you: Love one another. As I have loved you, so you must love one another. By this everyone will know that you are my disciples, if you love one another" (John 13:34-35 NIV).

How often, as an employee are we tempted to sluff off at work. But is this honorable? We may work while our boss is looking, but when his back is turned we slack off.

In *the way of love*, all slaves were instantly given a promotion. Rather than working for their earthly masters, they were promoted to being servants of their Almighty Lord.

Their current positions of servitude were simply a means to display the new way of love they were offering to the world. Their rewards were not given to them by their earthly masters. No, they were promised much more. Their reward came to them from the King of kings and their joy came from doing His work on Earth (Ephesians 6:5-8 NIV). And even their work ethic was seen as a means to reach the lost for Christ.

Then Paul turned his attention to the masters; what a truly dangerous position they are in. As believers, they are told to resist the corruption of fleshly power and, instead, reveal the way of love. If they cling too much to the natural power they are given, they can become corrupted and do great harm to their soul.

So, Paul admonishes them to treat their slaves well, because they really belonged to the Lord, reminding them of the One who truly has been given authority over all of us, slaves and masters equally. He said, "Do not threaten them, since you know that he who is both their Master and yours is in heaven, and there is no favoritism with him" (Ephesians 6:9 NIV). In essence, the masters were given an instant *demotion* by fleshly standards. And yet, it was truly a promotion as they were told they were servants to their Lord and Master.

It would seem from the outside looking in they were given a harsh sentence. But, truly, Paul liberated them from the danger of corruption. He gave them the grace of God, because it was a second chance at embracing the humility of the Lord and God gives

His grace to the humble (1 Peter 5:5).

In reality, Paul was teaching his disciples to live, not for this life, but as an investment in the next—to live with their minds set on eternity. This was their gift to the Father as well as a gift they give to themselves. For, truly, they would reap the rewards for their righteousness for all eternity!

Defining Submission

Submission is not the same as obedience. Submission is the *voluntary yielding* of one's self and ideas to another person. It cannot be demanded or forced, because it is not the same as obedience— voluntary indicates you have a choice.

Only slaves and children were told to obey, which is not voluntary. Obedience gives us no rights, whether male or female, but submission is a choice. We have the right to either submit or not, as guided by wisdom and conscience. If we are not using our wisdom and conscience to determine on a case by case basis whether to submit, then it is not voluntarily yielding, but it has become obedience.

If I tell my husband that I think our child needs to be grounded because of something he's done and my husband disagrees with me, he will express his feelings to me about it. Then, based on my reason and conscience I will either agree with his council or disagree. If I agree, then I have voluntarily yielded to his wisdom because I have seen that it is better. And obviously, that goes the other way as well. If my husband believes my reason is more sound, then he will defer to my council and thereby yield to it voluntarily.

If we demand submission, then we strip the other person of their reason and conscience and have then robbed them of their humanity. God gave both men and women brains and He wants us to use them.

I have often said, if we do not define submission when we preach about it, we should not preach about it. Because even as we mention it, every person defines it according to their own personal experience and sometimes those experiences are abusive and we inadvertently condone abuse.

I had a friend who found out that her 16 year old daughter was being sexually abuse by her husband and so she and her children left him. When my friend went to her pastor about the incident, she was told to go back to her husband and ask him to forgive her for leaving him. So, she did and her family was subsequently destroyed and all three of her children never spoke to her again.

What grieves me about this story is that as I have mentioned it to other evangelical ministers, they've continued to argue for blind obedience in marriage and have not been touched by the danger of it made obvious through the story of my friend. They seem to think nothing of the woman's humanity or of her children. No, it seems they only care to argue even at the expense of humanity.

Truly, their callous attitudes make me wonder about *their* humanity. If they can so easily throw out the human element for the sake of their argument, I believe they've lost touch with the Father. God, on the other hand, never loses touch with humanity. No, indeed, He has been present at every moment of every act of abuse and feels it keenly.

Sexist Jokes or Honor

"In the same way, you husbands must give *honor* to your wives. Treat your wife with understanding as you live together. She may be weaker (physically) than you are, but she is your equal partner in God's gift of new life. Treat her as you should so your prayers will not be hindered" (1 Peter 3:7 NLT emphasis mine).

In 2007, Sarah Palin ran as the republican vice-presidential candidate with John McCain. She was simply phenomenal and made a great splash in the political arena. Sarah terrified the opposition. So, strengthened by huge support from the vast majority of media outlets, they attacked her.

By far the most influential attack came from, believe it or not, SNL. Yes, Saturday Night Live made her the butt of every joke they possibly could. Her name was brought up in probably every episode through the rest of the campaign and she was subsequently maligned by humor. If you can make someone a joke it seems to be an acceptable form of slander or abuse and has a much greater effect on the way they are viewed than you would imagine.

Very similarly, the Greek playwrights used sexist jokes to denigrate women and build a platform for male dominance. By making anyone the brunt of a joke, you demean then and cause their dignity to be compromised. When we as women stop laughing at the jokes about women and call it what it is, men will stop laughing as well.

Obviously, mockery is not the way of love. It does not show honor or respect and, honestly, it's not funny.

II

Removing the Restraints

"Pursue righteousness and a godly life, along with faith, love, perseverance, and gentleness. Fight the good fight for the true faith" 1 Timothy 6:11-12 NLT.

THE GOAL OF Paul's first letter to Timothy was to aid Timothy in his defense of the church he led in Ephesus. The Ephesian church is one which Paul had started with Priscilla and her husband Aquila. This group of believers were simply being overrun by the witchcraft, pagan worship and debauchery that pervaded the city. Dark and wicked ideologies attacked the church from without and within.

In the church, a group of people began teaching twisted truths, mixing Christianity with other pagan beliefs amongst the Lord's people. We have to remember they did not have a local church building, but met in homes and Timothy, although the leader, was not the only teacher. As Christians met in homes, other teachers and teachings would arise and some of those teachings were false. We have a lot of this today as well.

The false teachings were so widespread that it seems Timothy was overwhelmed by them. We see in 1 Timothy 1:19-20 Paul tells Timothy to, *"Cling to your faith in Christ, and keep your conscience clear.*

For some people have deliberately violated their consciences; as a result their faith has been shipwrecked. Hymenaeus and Alexander are two examples. I threw them out and handed them over to Satan so they might learn not to blaspheme God."

Then he continues 1 Timothy 2:1-4, *"I urge you, first of all, to pray for all people. Ask God to help them; interceded on their behalf, and give thanks for them. Pray this way for kings and all who are in authority so that we can live peaceful and quiet lives marked by godliness and dignity. This is good and pleases God our Savior, who wants everyone to be saved and to understand truth"* (NLT).

Through these verses, we get the idea that what had attacked the Christians in Ephesus was very dark, almost overpowering and widespread. Paul tells Timothy to *"Cling to your faith in God!"* as if he were in jeopardy of falling prey to the erroneous teachings in the city. He then tells Timothy to URGE the people to pray for those caught in darkness. From the lowest to the highest king, Paul urges them to pray mercifully for those who were caught in error, and reminding him that God wants to save *everyone.* (v. 4).

I'm sure you'll agree, sometimes it is difficult to have mercy when you're in the middle of a battle and those attacking you are very wicked and hardhearted. Paul's main objective in the letter was to help save Ephesus and encourage Timothy to fight for truth in the city.

Harsh Language or Redemptive Teaching

1 Timothy 2 seems to have some of the harshest

language against women in the whole Bible and is a difficult passage to study. But it seemed that no matter how many other Scriptures I found to encourage my daughter or myself, reading this one seems to blow all the other proof away. It's as if a spell hangs over it and it has the power to hypnotize us into thinking we women are really just nothing. However, when studying it much deeper and clarifying some of the discrepancies, we see a much different truth emerge than what has historically been presented to us.

The NIV reads: *"Therefore I want the men everywhere to pray, lifting up holy hands without anger or disputing. I also want the women to dress modestly, with decency and propriety, adorning themselves, not with elaborate hairstyles or gold or pearls or expensive clothes, but with good deeds, appropriate for women who profess to worship God.*

A woman should learn in quietness and full submission. I do not permit a woman to teach or to assume authority over a man; she must be quiet. For Adam was formed first, then Eve. And Adam was not the one deceived; it was the woman who was deceived and became a sinner. But women will be saved through childbearing—if they continue in faith, love and holiness with propriety" 1 Timothy 2:8-15.

Now read the difference as presented by a David J. Hamilton, a Biblical scholar who wrote his master's thesis on these passages from his book *Why Not Women* written in accordance with the original Greek translation, and changes chosen to reflect the Greek grammar more accurately: *"I want men everywhere to lift up holy hands in prayer, with out of anger or disputing. Likewise, I want women to dress modestly, with decency and propriety, not with braided hair or gold or pearls or expensive clothes, but with good deeds, appropriate for women who profess to worship God.*

A woman should learn in quietness and full submission. I do not permit a woman to teach or to have authority over a man; she must be silent. For Adam was formed first, then Eve. And Adam was not the one deceived; it was the woman who was deceived and became a sinner. But she will be saved through the childbearing[1] Timothy 2:8-15.1 Virtually the same passage of Scripture, with only a few changes, made it much less devastating to woman.

So, was Paul telling Timothy to STOP women from preaching because they were too easily deceived? Paul was the champion for mercy, who'd established this very church with the help of Priscilla, a woman he greatly esteem. So, it is not likely that he's telling women to stop.

First of all, in 1 Timothy 2:8 Paul addresses the men and tells them to pray without anger or disputing. Obviously, they had been dealing with the errors in anger and argument instead of mercy and prayer. So, Paul addresses this and tells them to not get drawn in to harmful debates resulting in anger, losing the power of their witness, which is love. We have that same problem today. People think they can accomplish with human anger (James 1:20) what can only be accomplished by the Spirit. Yet, the main point Paul is making is a needed return to prayer, not debate.

Then, in 1 Timothy 2:9-10 Paul addresses the women of Ephesus and says, *likewise* or *also*. Paul's first word to the women was *likewise*, which in the

Greek is represented by an *ellipsis*, a literary equal sign, meaning that everything he has just told the men is implied to women also or LIKEWISE. Then he adds, *"I want women to dress modestly, with decency and propriety, not with braided hair or gold or pearls or expensive clothes but with good deeds, appropriate for women who profess to worship God."*

The city of Ephesus was wild with promiscuity, which was often associated with their pagan worship. The women who engaged in the pagan rituals dressed immodestly and ostentatiously—pearls and braids were associated with their style of dress. Paul wasn't saying pearls and braids were bad, but were, unfortunately, associated with the lifestyle of a promiscuous, pagan woman.

Paul wanted the Christian women to represent Christ in the way they dressed, while they PROFESSED (taught) their Christian beliefs. The word *professed* is important, but often overlooked in this passage. It obviously implies that Christian women were sharing their faith with unbelievers, as well as the church. Remember: there were NO pulpits then, just people sharing their faith and talking about Jesus.

So, Paul was telling the women of the Ephesus church to pray like he had asked the men to for the salvation of the pagan worshipers. He also asked them to dress differently from the pagans as an outward sign of their conversion to empower their witness.

All along, Paul's goal was to protect the witness of the believers in Ephesus. He was desperately in earnest for this because he had a passionate drive to reach people for Christ. That was his main life-goal and it never changed. He wanted to engage all people, both men and women, in winning souls through every possible means. He used the gender inclusive term *anthropos*, (meaning: a human being, whether male or female) consistently when referring to women winning souls, because he wanted every warrior he could get his hands on! He did not excluded women in or outside the church from sharing and teaching if they were qualified teachers, because he needed laborers.

False Teacher

In 1 Timothy 2:11-15, Paul talks about an unnamed woman in the church who had been deceived by the false doctrines spreading through Ephesus. Although, she was in the church, her teachings were most likely a mixture of the cultural pagan beliefs and Christianity—a twisted version of the truth Paul felt was detrimental to the believers there.

He addresses the issue Timothy was having with her by saying, *"A woman should learn in quietness and full submission. I do not permit a woman to teach or to assume authority over a man; she must be quiet. For Adam was formed first, then Eve. And Adam was not the one deceived; it was the woman who was deceived and became a sinner. But she will be save through [the] childbearing."* 1 Timothy 2:11-15 NIV (emphasis mine).

Some scholars believe the above mentioned passage was added after the fact and was not in the original text. But even if it was original, its meaning has been marred by translators and cultural differences.

Many scholars agree that Paul was not addressing these comments to ALL women in Ephesus, but just ONE woman. We know this because in the Greek all the plural nouns are gone in verses 11:15, he stopped speaking in generalities, "everyone, men, women" and changed to a singular noun, a *woman*. Everywhere else, when speaking of *women* he says women but here he changes to the singular use of a *woman*.

Paul chooses not to name the woman who was caught up in deception, because he hopes to win her over to right theology. You see, Paul believed the only antidote for deception was truth and he wanted to dissuade her from error to the truth. He says in v. 11, she (the woman he mentioned) "should learn in quietness and full submission." Paul wanted this woman taught correctly.

We understand through many of his letters this was a theme he revisited often—teaching women the Scriptures. Women were vulnerable to deception *only* due to their lack of knowledge, because they were previously forbidden to learn the Scriptures - this was a travesty to Paul.

He wanted this ONE women to be taught and Paul further instructed her to learn in *quietness* and *submission*; quiet, meaning a teachable attitude and compliance with the truths being taught. For her to learn she would have to fully submit to the teachings she learned and not mix them with pagan beliefs. She would need to voluntarily give up her erroneous thinking in exchange for the instruction she would receive from other qualified Christian teachers.

When Paul says, "I do not permit a woman to teach," he is saying that in regards to the ONE

115

woman who was teaching erroneously because she was not qualified. Until she had learnt *the way of salvation* correctly, she would not be allowed to teach.

Paul's ultimate goal for this woman was to make her a qualified PROFESSOR of the truth; that was his goal, not to silence her permanently, just until she was qualified or had learned the truth. Jewish scholars always connected learning with teaching, the latter being the end result of learning. Otherwise, what was the use of teaching them?

Women had been previously forbidden to learn because the men didn't want them to be qualified teachers. The only reason this ONE woman was forbidden from teaching was because she was teaching false doctrine and Paul wanted the doctrine stopped, not women.

Earlier, Paul told Timothy to remember the teachings of his grandmother, Lois, and his mother, Eunice, who Paul knew to be great teachers of *the way*, in order to guide him through the deception he was encountering in Ephesus. So, do we really think that now he was telling women NOT to teach, when he made it clear women had taught Timothy as well as himself. Or was he saying it was okay for a woman to teach a man in private, but not to speak publicly?

Remember there were no public church buildings at this time. All teachings were done in homes or outside in secret places. People would gather together and basically have a Bible study without a Bible. Teachers taught from what they learned or from teachings that had been passed down to them. So, it's very likely Lois and Eunice were strategic in Timothy's training, as they taught *the way of salvation* out of their homes.

So, imagine women were the care-takers of the home and they were opening up their homes for Christians to meet together and share, but then they were being told *not to speak in their own homes.* This doesn't sound right to me.

When Paul says, "*I do not permit a woman to teach or to assume authority over a man,*" again, he was talking about the same woman, that she should not be allowed to have authority. The word *authority* in this Scripture is murky and difficult to translate. Because it was so seldom used in the new testament, there is very little to reference it with. Maybe this woman had been usurping Timothy's authority and that is why he added that phrase. But by any translation, Paul was only referring to this one woman and only until she could be taught properly, because she was not above reproach.

Then Paul mentions Eve and says, "*For Adam was formed first, then Eve. And Adam was not the one deceived; it was the woman who was deceived and became a sinner*" (1 Timothy 2: 13-14 NLT).

First of all, you have to realize that through a study of Paul's letters you can determined that he had great compassion for Eve. He believed she had been deceived because she was not taught correctly what God had told Adam. Adam had allowed her to be deceived while he stood by and watched her, finally ·joining her with a clear understanding of what he was doing and was not deceived as Eve was (Genesis 3:6).

If you understand Paul's personality you could image how he would have reacted to this wrong he felt had been done to Eve by Adam. It may be the reason Paul felt such compassion for the ONE woman who had taught false doctrine, because he believed so strongly in women being taught correctly and not left to their own devises, making them vulnerable to *old wives tales* (1 Timothy 4:7). So, when Paul connects this ONE woman with Eve, to him it is not an insult, but he connected her with feelings of understanding and compassion he had for Eve.

Some scholars believe Paul may have been refuting a false doctrine circulating at the time in Ephesus—an exaggerated version of creation which taught that women were the SOURCE of men and were, therefore, head or ruler over them. In referencing the fall, he may have been addressing the teaching this ONE woman had circulated. In stating, *men were made first*, he was refuting gender bias, with a statement of gender equality, as he had done in previous letters.

By saying "*Adam was formed first, then Eve,*" he wasn't saying men were better or smarter, but was just refuting a false doctrine that had been spreading. Remember, Paul had said earlier in (1 Corinthians 11:11 NLT), "*But among the Lord's people, women are not independent of men, and men are not independent of women*" teaching that men and women were not independent from each other.

In 1 Timothy 2:14, Paul says, "But she will be saved through the childbearing." This sounds demeaning, as if he were saying the only thing women are good for is making babies. But he was not referring to *childbearing*. We know this because he did not say childbearing, but, in the Greek it says, *the childbearing*. Timothy knew what Paul referred to so Paul did not need to define what he meant when he said it. He was referring to THE CHILD—the Christ child in Genesis 3:15. If Paul was really saying, "Women gain salvation through childbearing," this would nullify the work of Christ.

Referencing the creation story again, the childbearing was a reference to God's promised Savior. *"I will put enmity Between you and the woman, And between your seed and her seed; He shall bruise you on the head, And you shall bruise him on the heel."* (NASB)

Genesis 3:15 *is* God's plan of salvation, and in it He was prophesying the coming of the Christ child as well as the destruction of Satan. She, meaning Eve, or all women, would eventually be Satan's downfall! The woman Satan had deceived would bring truth into the world. It would be she who would be the vessel heaven would use to overtake the rule of the prince of darkness. The victory of her seed was the vengeance of the woman—her victory over her deceiver, her justification.

Again, Paul was asking for the same compassion for this ONE woman that they felt Eve deserved and reminding Timothy that the ONE woman in question, too, needed redemption. Remember, Paul, above all things, was a soul-winner. Even when he brought correction, it was to save their souls. So we see, Paul wanted her saved, not silence!

It is difficult to understand the harsh language used in this passage, but if we view it in the light of culture and translation, we can more clearly understand why it seems to contradict the rest of Paul's teachings about women. He wasn't unsaying or changing his mind about women, but he was misinterpreted and misunderstood. Through knowledge of changes in culture, difficulties facing the Ephesus church and translation choices, we can see it much more clearly.

Women Leaders

Paul continues to bring a message of equality for both genders in 1Timothy 3:1-13. He says, "*If someone (anyone) aspires to be an elder, he desires an honorable position.*" He continued, giving qualifications for elders in the church in order to see that those who teach are those who understand and live the Gospel well. Paul did not want new believers teaching because they might fall into the same deception as the ONE woman he'd just referenced.

The important verses in chapter 3 are 11-13, in which Paul says, likewise or, in the same way, women should be held by the same standards as the men which he'd just mentioned, before becoming leaders and teachers in the church.

Some translations use the word wives instead of the word *women*. The word used in the Greek was *gune*, which can be translated either wives or women. In choosing to translate the word as *wives*, they have slanted its meaning, making it sound like Paul was only referring to the wives of the ministers, not actual women ministers. Their choice of words when translating uncovers bias against women, but does not reveal Paul's true heart or line up with the rest of what he said about women in ministry.

Paul wrote gune and meant it to mean women, not wives. We know this because Paul consistently used the gender inclusive terms when writing to the church, referring to Christians of both genders which is consonant with the rest of his behavior toward women.

If Paul wanted to stop women ministers, why in 1 Timothy 3:11 would he set up guidelines for women ministers?

We have to remember that Paul spent a great deal of time with the churches he started. The vast majority of what he taught them was in verbal form and we can never know everything he taught them. We have only his written letters which give us just a taste of what he taught. In much of the letters, he refers to what he's taught them audibly when he was with them. He references it knowing that they already had an understanding of what he was communicating. He didn't give an in depth explanation because they already had an understanding of what he was implying.

In understanding Paul's letters, we have to keep in mind his *actions* as well, and compare them with what he wrote. It is wrong to assume we know what he meant *and erase his character* with a few verses he wrote; it's wrong to him as well as to those it affects. To be fair, we need to dig deep and embrace the full meaning of what was said. If we don't, we are no better than the false teachers Paul is referring to in his letters.

(1) Why Not Women, Lauren Cunningham and David Joel Hamilton, 208

12

Honoring God's Word

"Love is patient, love is kind. It does not envy, it does not boast, it is not proud. It does not dishonor others, it is not self-seeking..." 1 Corinthians 13:4-5 NIV.

THERE IS NO easy explanation for 1 Corinthians 14:34 which states, "Women should be silent during the church meetings. It is not proper for them to speak. They should be submissive, just as the law says" (NLT). If it were easy to understand, we would not have Christians in an uproar over it for centuries. To those who quote it and use it as proof that women should not minister, I say, please, read the whole Bible!

If you read this verse and this verse only, you may agree with those who've used it to keep women from walking in obedience to their callings, but you can never or should never read one verse without taking into consideration all the verses before and after it. Nor should you use one verse to negate the rest of the Bible, in which we are given countless examples of powerful women ministers. (Exodus 15:20; Judges 4:4; 2 Kings 22:14; Esther 1-8; Luke 8:1-3; Luke 2:36; Luke 10:38-42; John 4:27-38; Luke 1:26-38; Acts 9:36-42; Acts 16:13-15; Romans 16:3; 2 Timothy 1:5, just to name a few)

If you read the entire passage in 1 Corinthians, you would conclude that Paul could not possibly be telling the church women shouldn't minister. On the contrary, in the same passage he continually talks about women prophesying. As Paul teaches them *how* they should use the gift of prophesy (a ministry gift), He continually addresses both men and women as his "brothers and *sisters*," instructing them about prophecy throughout the letter.

In light of Paul's previous teaching of the way of love, you can see that the traditional teaching used to silence women stands in stark contrast to what else he has taught about the equality of Christianity. Throughout his ministry, Paul strove continually to build up and promote women in ministry. He was probably the biggest promoter of women in ministry second only to Jesus. He often praised the women he worked with to others, expressing their valuable service to the kingdom. Again and again, he referred to women as his co-workers in the same way he referenced his relationships with his male counterparts.

Throughout his letters, he praised the work of Priscilla, Lydia, Phoebe, Lois, Eunice, Junia, Tryphena, Tryphosa, Persis, Julia, Olympus and Mary. And there are many other accounts of the women Paul ministered and worked with that did not make it into the Scriptures, yet, are referenced in historical documents.

Robbing the Church

It seems absolutely crazy to think that Paul, of all people, was telling women to stop ministering. For those who see him that way I say, you do not understand Paul's ministry. He's not in one of y'all's good old boys' club, whipping a high hat to macho men everywhere. No way! He wasn't a "man's man" by today's definition—he was an *unapologetic Jesus boy*!

I would like to stop here and say that, as a woman, the mishandling of this passage and others like it has caused great pain to women throughout time. It not only causes pain to have ones gender singled out and demoted as if God created you to be mistreated, second class or subhuman, but simply put, it hurts... a lot. Honestly, most men do not understand what it feels like to have their humanity questioned. It is ultimately destabilizing and it leads to more questions than it answers.

In essence, if woman is proven to be sub-human, then our next question will have to be: How human is she? By even giving rise to the question of a woman's humanity, you open a door for the depravity of mankind to overtake her and we are ultimately led to the reasoning that procures prostitution and the trafficking of women.

God created husband and wife to be ONE. If woman is less than man then they are no longer ONE, but 3/4 or less. If woman is subhuman then it is up to humanity to determine by mere opinion how human she is? And history, unfortunately, has proven that opinion cannot be relied upon and can sink to the lowest forms of degradation.

Our conscience is a God-given force inside every human that tells us when we're off course. If listened to, it will keep us right, but unfortunately it is not always heeded. So, what can we rely on to aid our conscience? We have truth, and in this instance our truth would be the *equal humanity of women*. If we take one step away from that truth, we will find ourselves at the mercy of conscience and due to human wickedness, our conscience can too easily fail us unless governed by truth.

Our conscience (moral compass) or our opinions cannot guide us in our estimation of women's value (equality), it must be God and God alone. And He says, "God created human beings in his own image. In the image of God he created them; male and female he created them" (Genesis 1:27 NLT).

The very human opinions of mankind have caused pain, grief and torment—yes, torment throughout history. For, though obviously anointed and gifted by the Holy Spirit, women have been told it was sinful for them to preach or teach about the God they loved. As a woman in ministry, I have been confronted by men and women who believe I am going to hell because I am a woman preacher. They seem to have absolutely no empathy of what it feels like to be treated like a malady. I have to question their motives and ask, do they really believe they will redeem me and save my soul through their hateful attitudes? It's sad, really, and not redemptive—quite the opposite, actually.

It feels horrible to be singled out and treated so badly simply because you feel a calling to tell others about the God you love. Honestly, their logic is so twisted I find it hard to believe they serve the God I know. Because the God I love dearly loves me and has chosen to share His heart with me. He made me a woman—that is no accident! He chose me and raised me up to share His heart. Yet, they try to convince me that my God does not like me and doesn't approve of me and all He has shared with me is a lie.

For centuries, the enemy has used Scripture to subvert God's plans—it is not a new thing—he even tried it with Jesus. We have to understand that this is a part of the battle we face. Indeed, it's quite shrewd of the enemy to use Scripture to generate a rivalry between the genders, pitting them against each other, causing one to tear down the work of the other. If I were him, that's what I would do!

If I were the devil, I would try to convince over 50% of the church they were not supposed to share the gospel. Even by creating a distinction, he's created a divide, causing one half to demean and ridicule the other half. If you see it from Satan's point of view, it is a marvelously witty strategy.

Indeed, we are commanded to pray for laborers for the harvest. Does that apply only to male workers? Did Jesus say, "Pray for *male* workers for the harvest?" No, it's not gender specific. It's simple. He said, "The harvest is plentiful, but the workers are few. Ask the Lord of the harvest, therefore, to send out workers into his harvest field" (Luke 10:2 NIV). Paul constantly stated "brothers and sisters" on purpose, to fix it in their minds both genders were included.

Truly, as a church, we are not being very intelligent. By buying into this scheme, we have robbed ourselves of half our labor force, simply because we have fallen prey to personal bias and religious bigotry. However, it is a smart strategy for the kingdom of darkness to use in attempting to stop the spread of the gospel. The harvest field is ready and now, truly, more than ever we need laborers—it's time to reassess our imposed qualifications for ministry.

Learning Ministry

In the culture of Paul's time, many born-again Christians were coming out of pagan religions, so their attitudes were affected by what was esteemed in their pagan ceremonies. These customs were naturally transferred to the new religion they were learning.

In most pagan religions, the more chaotic, noisy and uproarious their worship was, the more devoted they were thought to be. In many of their religions, they engaged professional worshipers who were very loud and noisy and were usually always women. Perhaps you've heard of the wailing women from pagan religious ceremonies—it was their job to worship their gods ostentatiously.

As Paul was introducing prophesy to the new church, it's easy to see how things could get a little crazy. With all new believers in a brand new religion, they were birthing a completely new way of thinking into society. He had to actually tell them, "For God is not a God of disorder but of peace" (1 Corinthians 14:33 NIV) because they weren't used to that. He told them, you can control yourself, for "The spirits of prophets are subject to the control of prophets" (1 Corinthians 14:32NIV. They weren't used to that either. It was essential they realize the purpose of prophesy was to build up the believers, (1 Corinthians 14:32), not to put on a show.

Most importantly, he wanted them to keep the ultimate goal of love in the forefront of their minds. Love should be used to guard their conduct in ministry and all they were doing in the church. Christ's command to love, should guide ministers most of all, since we exemplify the kingdom of heaven. Paul was striving to bring needed order to the way women and men conducted themselves in ministry, summed up by the law of love.

Paul's order for women to be silent in 1 Corinthians 14:34, was first spoken to those who spoke in tongues (1 Corinthians 14:28) and then also to those who prophesied (v. 30). He was not, in either of those instances, telling either group to be silent in all churches forever—just when others were ministering. It was just instruction to keep their meetings orderly and to not be like the heathens, who were the exact opposite in their worship.

Simply said, there's a time for women to speak (in church), a time to speak in tongues (in church), and a time for prophesy (in church). At those times, it is good for men and women to minister and develop their gifts in order to edify the church.

We should use the previous chapter of the letter, 1 Corinthians 13, to govern our behavior in worship, tongues and prophesy—*all should be done in love*. Often referred to as the love chapter, it gives us explicit instructions to guide all aspect of life, including worship and ministry for both men and women.

If we remember, Paul was writing a letter addressing issues that had been brought to his attention. He was answering questions brought to him by those seeking guidance in the issues facing the church in Corinth. Their services were not like ours are, where only a handful of people speak to a congregation of believers. No, in their meetings, every believer, both male and female, were instructed to bring a hymn, or a word of instruction, a revelation, a tongue or an interpretation to share with the church (1 Corinthians 14:26).

In realizing the confusion that had been brought about by the *new* gifts they were given, ie. tongues, prophesy and women in ministry (yes, women are a gift to the church), Paul sought to guide the new believers. Obviously, they had never experienced tongues before and prophesy in the old covenant was saved for "special" people, not the common church goer. And of course, women for the first time had been allowed to be a part of their worship service. Previously, women were relegated to the outer court. Now, they were in the same service as the men and were suddenly allowed to study the Scriptures (Torah), which had formerly been forbidden to them.

So, if you can imagine, *perhaps* Paul received a letter from one of the churches he started, expressing their confusion and seeking guidance. They may have even stated what actions they had taken so far to control the situation. In their letter to Paul, they *may* have quoted the teachings of others who forbid women speaking in church because it had become chaotic. (Sounds like the reaction in many churches).

Paul answers by saying first in verse 34, "Women should be silent during the church meetings. It is not proper for them to speak. They should be submissive, just as the law says" (1 Corinthians 14:34 NLT). It sounds like he's unsaying what he had said previously, which was to see women released in the churches (see 1 Corinthians 14:1 & 39, Romans 16:1-2, 1 Timothy 2:9).

However, if we compare this verse to his answers

about tongues and prophesy, you can see that he wasn't meaning for women to be silent in church and never to speak again. But just as with prophesy, his "be silent," from the Greek word hésuchazó meaning: *rest from work, cease from altercation, am silent, live quietly or lead a quiet life*, was a guide to heart behavior.

He was asking them to wait their turn. This lines up with what else he said previously in 1 Corinthians 14:26-33, to be silent (be still) while others are speaking and wait your turn so it is not disorderly and everyone is benefited by what you have to say.

In 1 Corinthians 14, Paul was requiring both men and women to have a *submissive heart-attitude* toward everyone in their meetings, not to fight and try to be heard above everyone else. In order to display love for one another, they would have to have a gentle, meek, submissive attitude toward one another, preferring the other above themselves (Romans 12:10). "Do nothing out of selfish ambition or vain conceit. Rather, in humility value others above yourselves" (Philippians 2:3 NIV).

Again, *this attitude of rest* teaching reinforces his instructions on possessing and ministering with an attitude of submission. Paul is reiterating what he said earlier: that women should continue ministering in an *attitude of submission*, as he stated in Ephesian 5:21—they should all "submit to one another" or to be subject to one another.

He is not saying women alone should submit to the law, but women should be taught to submit to the same law men do, which is the law of love.

You see, the Greek Jews who wrote the Septuagint (the Greek version of the Hebrew Scriptures), used the word submission as a parallel for being silent before God. They used the word to imply that one should submit oneself to God first and foremost above any human being. Their first rule was to surrender to the leading and guidance of God, therefore submitting and relinquishing their lives to Him.

Remember, the focus of Paul's letter was to reinforce the law of love that was first established as the *new commandment* (John 13:34), that took precedence over every other teaching. So, here we see again Paul simply restating what he said previously in the letter that love is the most important law and should come first in ministry. Women, as well as men, are commanded to submit to one another, attaining an attitude of submission as the law of love commands (Ephesians 5:21), submitting first to God, then submitting to others as unto God.

Another misunderstanding about this Scripture has risen in the church simply because few people truly understand the meaning of submission. It does not mean obey as a child or slave is commanded to obey (Ephesians 6:1, 6:5), but the word hypotásso is best described as *yielding voluntarily*—it is a choice. And hupakoé literally means "*submission* to what is *heard*," not to be a hearer only but a doer as well. By yielding to others and considering them before ourselves we choose to act in humility and God gives His *grace* to the *humble*, either male or female.

Love-guided Ministry

Paul went on to give them further guidance to their problem when he says, "If they want to inquire about something, they should ask their own husbands at home" (1 Corinthians 14:35 NIV). This is actually a very remarkable statement Paul is making. He is saying "if" the women want to learn they should ask their husbands...this is a shake-the-earth revolutionary statement!

Seriously, in their culture, what Paul was really saying to them was unheard of—it was mind blowing! Paul, a teacher, apostle and religious leader, is actually telling husbands to *teach their wives* if they choose to learn. He wanted men to teach their wives and share the revelation they'd received with them. The simple act of sharing and teaching would show the world how valuable women are. By telling the men to teach their wives, he is contradicting the traditional, erroneous teachings which forbid men to teach women the Pentateuch (Hebrew Scriptures).

In the Greek and Roman societies, women had few opportunities to learn and in Judaism, the rabbis taught that it was a shame for a man (husband, father or brother) to teach his wives, daughters or sisters about the Torah or other Jewish writings. But, in Christianity, it would be quite different!

Paul blew the doors off women learning to minister! He's instructed men to teach their wives if they chose to learn. He was not only telling women it's okay to learn, but that husbands have an obligation to teach them. He was commanding husbands to mentor their wives in the Scriptures. Wow!

Instead of shutting down the women or demeaning them, he's done quite the opposite—He wants them to be taught! He wanted them to have an understanding of the Scriptures, because it was a shame the rabbis had previously forbidden women to be taught.

Also, another thing we must understand about this passage is in Paul's time there were no punctuations in writing, so, we don't really know when one thought ends and another begins. At the end of verse 35, it states that it is a "disgraceful" thing for women to speak in church. What scholars have wrestled with for centuries is the existence of a small word right after it which is what they call an *emotional rebuttal* for what was just said—indicating a counterargument.

For instance, many scholars believe Paul was quoting a teaching that was not his own, such as "It is disgraceful for a women to speak in church" (1 Corinthians 14:35 NIV). Then he answered what he had quoted with an emotional rebuttal, arguing against it saying, "It is disgraceful (or improper) for women to speak in church? Nonsense!" or "What?" or "No way!" Then he states the opposite of the quote he just stated which is, "Do you think the word of God originated with you?" Here he has another emotional rebuttal, such as "What!" So, it may read "What! Are you the *only* people it has reached?"

Similarly, if you wanted to quote something you disagreed with like, "Pigs can fly," and then said, "Phewy," there's just no way to translate it. So, Paul's emotional rebuttal has been simply left out of translations for centuries.

What has increased the confusion of this passage of the letter is that there were no quotation marks to show he's actually quoting a previous theology and not stating it himself. During this letter, Paul has repeatedly quoted others such as: the Old Testament Scriptures, the words of Jesus (Luke 22:19-20), the

Greek dramatist Menander (Thais), rabbinic prophesy (B. Makkot 23a) and other believers (1 Corinthians 1:12, 3:4, 6:12-13, 10:23, 12:3, 15:35) and non-believers (1 Corinthians 10:28, 12:3, 14:25). That, coupled with his use of the mark indicating an emotional rebuttal, show that he isn't contradicting his previous teaching on the release of women into ministry positions (1 Corinthians 14:26; also Romans 16:1), but actually reiterating it.

After voicing his rebuttal of the quoted concepts, he concludes this thought by immediately restating his conclusions in verse 39 that both men and women were to prophesy. He says, "So, my dear brothers and sisters, be eager to prophesy, and don't forbid speaking in tongues. But (or just) be sure that everything is done properly and in order" (1 Corinthians 14:39-40).

Love Does NOT Demand its Own Way!

Truly, Paul has not wavered from his letter's main goal, which is to bring clarification to the new way of love he has introduced to them. In the previous chapter, 1 Corinthians 13, he's already stated what should be the law that governs them all and that is the law of love.

"Love is patient, love is kind. It does not envy, it does not boast, it is not proud. It does not dishonor others, it is not self-seeking..." Love does not demand its own way! 1 Corinthians 13:4-5 NIV.

Love is patient and allows others adequate time to share what God has placed on their hearts.

Love is kind and *appreciates* the contributions others make to the ministry of the church.

Love doesn't envy and give way to the natural insecurities in our hearts, yet honors without fearing others might get more than we do—responding to their ministry in a way that would build them up to bring even greater ministry through their lives.

Love does not boast and is not proud; it doesn't think of self (or at least it fights the instincts to consider the ways, thoughts and inclinations of self).

Love does not dishonor either women or men who are sharing their heart by interrupting them while they're speaking.

Love puts others first, and seeks to draw the best from them.

Love is not self-seeking, it does not demand or dominate, but encourages. Love protects, esteems and builds up—it does not control, hate or dominate!

It does not target one sex and demean them in the name of God, reducing their life's meaning to a subservient, underprivileged human. On the contrary, love protects their equality and strives to convince them of their worth and value in Christianity in whatever capacity God calls them to.

God is raising up a last-days army of believers who will be guided by love to protect the humanity of all people. As we embrace the teachings of Christ and Paul, we will be embracing the call of the army of the Lord. Any areas of our heart where hatred and prejudice dwell will make us vulnerable. So, seek the armor of love and you will made invincible.

13

Army Of Women

"Kings and armies flee in haste; the women at home divide the plunder" Psalm 68:12 NIV.

AFTER I'D BEEN praying, prophesying and believing God for revival for years, the Father asked me one day, "What kind of revival do you want?"

Knowing full-well His questions are usually leading questions, I asked Him, "Well, what kind of revival should I want, Father?"

He answered back, "Do you want a revival of *souls* or of *miracles*?"

I thought for a bit and answered, "I would like a revival of souls... *with* a lot of miracles!"

"How many souls do you want?" He continued.

Digging deep for an answer, I remembered Evan Roberts from the historical Welsh revival asked God for 100,000 souls and he got them. So, I hesitantly answered, "Could I have 100,000 souls, Lord?"

He was silent.

I knew I had answered timidly, so I tried again. Reaching for more faith, I answered, "500,000 souls, Lord?"

Again, I heard nothing.

I knew I was not believing for enough from Him

and tried again. "1,000,000 souls, Lord?" I asked sheepishly.

Again, nothing. I tried again, "5,000,000?"

Nothing.

Wow! I really thought I was led by faith with that last guess, so I just threw caution to the wind and declared loudly, "One-billion souls, Lord!"

"Now you are talking, daughter," He answered.

Later, I questioned Him, "Lord, how could *I* win a billion souls?"

That is when He showed me His simple equation for exponential revival. He said, "All you need to start with is 5,000 people, sold out and equipped to redeem the harvest."

If those 5000 people each led only 3 people to the Lord, that would be 15,000, turning it over only 5 times, you would already be at 1 million people, and that is only the beginning. I saw it all as He laid out His plan in my spirit. With only 5,000 awakened believers, I could win one billion souls.

So, when I think of you, dear friend, reading this book and walking in the liberty of the Father's value, I don't see you alone—I see 1 billion souls coming to Jesus through you!

A Great Light

One night as I slept, I was awakened by the Lord as His presence filled the room. Suddenly, I saw myself sitting in my little home, safe and snuggling, spending precious time with Jesus. As I continued to watch the vision unfold, I saw myself get up from my comfy chair and dart out into the dark chill of the night. Guided by one small torch, I felt compelled to venture into the night to try and light the way for the lost, whom I *knew* in my heart were trying desperately to find their way home.

As I stood atop a lone dark hill, I raised up my torch as high as I could. In the hope the lost would see its light, I held it for them to find their way in the darkness. Off in the distance, a group of wolves laughed at my little light and mocked my faith, "They will never see your puny light, girl."

I knew they were right in that my light wasn't much, but it was all I could do for them. So, I held it as high as I could for as long as I could stand it. Off in the distance, hidden by a thick covering of woods, I sensed the lost, too afraid to come to the light. Bolstered by the penetrating night, the wolves taunted them with their contempt as the heavy darkness blocked their way home.

Anger rose inside me in response to the audacity of the haughty wolves. It was terribly dark, yet their apathy enraged me. Throwing my head back, closing my eyes and looking toward heaven, I cried out to God, "Make my light brighter, Lord!"

When I opened my eyes, I saw the entire hillside was lit up with a great light. As I looked around, it was literally covered with a large crowd of women and many good men all holding their torches high into the night's sky to guide the lost home.

King David prophesied of a great host of women victorious in battle, "The Lord announces the word (Divine utterance), and the women who proclaim it are a mighty throng: '*Kings and armies flee in haste; the women at home divide the plunder!*'" (Psalm 68:11-12 NIV emphasis mine).

God Will Bring the Victory to YOU!

The enemy has tried desperately to limit the effectiveness of women, but, just like Jael in Judges 4:17-24, if the enemy keeps you from going to war, God will bring the victory to you. So, *let* the enemy underestimate you. By underestimating you, he's just given you the keys to destroy him. He's placed you in just the right position to ruin him.

Deborah was a prophet who governed the entire nation of Israel while Sisera lead King Jabin's army against Israel. One day she called for Barak to lead the armies of Israel in battle against the Canaanite king. She said to him, "This is what the Lord, the God of Israel, commands you: Call out 10,000 warriors from the tribes of Naphtali and Zebulun at Mount Tabor. And I will call out Sisera, commander of Jabin's army, along with his chariots and warriors, to the Kishon River. There I will give you victory over him." (Judges 4:6-7 NLT).

Yet, despite Deborah's assurance of victory, Barak refused to go against Sisera unless Deborah agreed to go with him (Judges 4:8). Deborah agreed to go with the army, but prophesied that because of his lack of faith, he would receive no honor from the victory God would give them. Instead, she said, "The Lord's victory over Sisera will be at the hands of a woman" (Judges 4:9 NLT).

That woman was Jael. She was at home in her tent, but God brought the battle to her.

When Barak attacked, God caused Sisera and his men to run in panic. Looking for an escape, "Sisera ran to the tent of Jael, the wife of Heber the Kenite, because Heber's family was on friendly terms with

King Jabin of Hazor. Jael went out to meet Sisera and said to him, 'Come into my tent, sir. Come in. Don't be afraid.' So he went into her tent, and she covered him with a blanket.

'Please give me some water,' he said. 'I'm thirsty.' So she gave him some milk from a leather bag and covered him again.

'Stand at the door of the tent,' he told her. 'If anybody comes and asks you if there is anyone here, say no.'

But when Sisera fell asleep from exhaustion, Jael quietly crept up to him with a hammer and tent peg in her hand. Then she drove the tent peg through his temple and into the ground, and so he died.

When Barak came looking for Sisera, Jael went out to meet him. She said, 'Come, and I will show you the man you are looking for.' So he followed her into the tent and found Sisera lying there dead, with the tent peg through his temple" (Judges 4:17-22 NLT).

Jael was probably the last one that Barak considered would win the battle for Israel that day, but God chose her for that very reason. God was sending us a message: We cannot limit Him! He refuses to be put in a box! Tell Him He can't do something and that is just what He will do. Give Him a desert and He'll make a forest (Isaiah 41:19). Give Him a housewife and He'll make her a warrior. This is God's heart concerning you. He sees beyond our weaknesses and sees a victorious warrior.

Who are You?

When I first began to write, a good friend of mine offered to show my writings to an editor of a major publication. Of course I was delighted...until I heard back from her. The editor thought my writing was good, but implied I was a nobody, with no influence. "Who is she," the editor asked my good friend, "to tell me how to live..." It hit me like a brick and for another ten years I wrote nothing. I listened to her words and let them define me.

Ten years later, God showed me a vision for my writing. I saw a simple notebook full of prophetic words the Lord gave me and from the center of the page four silvery white birds suddenly appeared and flew out from the pages. I watched as I saw the birds fly all over the world—from an African hut, to the elaborate rooms of a palace and pulpits all over the globe. The Father promised me, "If you obey Me, I will carry your words all over the world."

I was simply in shock and fought hard to even believe what God showed me, but I obeyed Him and wrote. God fulfilled His promise to me and He has literally taken my simple words all over the world.

It began simply, as I was home raising my children, but it didn't take long before I was covering the world with His messages of hope. God brought the battle to me! I was just a simple housewife, yet from this humble beginning the Lord has given me the possibility of reaching the world. He has sent His messages "throughout the earth, and (His) words to all the world" (Psalm 19:4 NLT, emphasis mine).

Victorious Women in Revivals

Crowds were astonished during the Welsh revival in 1905 when revivalist Evan Roberts allowed women to lead in the services he held. These women were breaking new ground just by singing and preaching. Even the most reserved persons were captivated by the passion these women had for God. What most people did not know is women had helped birth the revival; alongside Roberts, they labored in prayer to see the manifestation of God's presence.

William J. Seymour, was another who led an army of women in revival, in which both blacks and whites worked together enjoying the presence of the Holy Spirit. In the Spirit's presence, it seemed that discrimination had dissolved between the races. In throngs of hungry, passionate seekers, position and gender prejudices vanished as well. As they did, heaven came down in the little chapel in Los Angeles, CA from 1906-1909 in what is called the Azuza Street Revival.

Men and women from all the ranks of society worshiped joyfully in the old building on Azuza Street. The former stable for horses hosted hundreds of believers who would lay basking in God's presence on the old dirt floor.

Alongside each other, they felt His overwhelming presence equally, with no deference made for their gender, race or social standing. By the social standards of their day, they had very little in common except their deeply held passionate hunger for God. Gathered together, they epitomized the kingdom of heaven.

Furthermore, in both the first and second great awakenings, women labored and interceded to bring in the harvest. The Second Great Awakening especially effected the lives of women. The majority of people converted were women who also played a crucial role in the awakening's advancement and direction. Many husbands actually demanded their wives chose between their religious activities and their marriage.

Revivalist Charles Finney recognized the power of women's ministry and knew their role in the revival was crucial. He often called upon women to lead in prayer publicly. He saw that without the role of women, it would have been much harder for the revival's effectiveness to be realized.

The Second Great Awakening (1825-1835) produced many reform movements that continued to develop for centuries to come. Many prominent and well-informed female-lead organizations, responsible for many of the evangelical converts, were birthed through the awakening. These organizations propelled the movement's focus toward social activism and reform. Of these, the American Bible Society and the Temperance Movement were the most well-known.

Most notably, the Second Great Awakening birthed the movement for women's rights, as well as the abolitionist movement. These movements were founded on belief in the Word of God—that all men, as well as all women, were created equally by God!

Beguines Women

Even more remarkable, and one of my favorite revival occurrences regarding women, is the account of the Beguines women in the thirteenth century. In the low countries of Northern Europe during the middle ages, marriageable men were scarce, leaving many single women of middle class.

During this time in history, women were allowed only two honorable roles in society in which they could serve God: becoming a nun or running a household as a wife. However, for a young woman wanting to serve God, joining a convent was very expensive and if her family could not afford the dowry the church required, there was no other way for her to serve. That is, until the brave Beguines women broke the mold.

Living alone, these women devoted their lives to prayer and serving the poor. Finally, forming communities of women vowing to live a consecrated life to God, they performed good works and took care of each other.

Their communities flourished as they sought an intimate relationship with God and devoted themselves to religious work. Before long, men as well as women sought out these communities to sit under the powerful teachings of Beguines women, such as Marie of Oignies. A leading teacher of the Beguines movement, Marie of Oignies encountered many visions, experiencing ecstasy (a sudden change in perception due to direct contact with Holy Spirit), and wept uncontrollably as she reflected on the crucifixion of Christ.

The shift toward Christian mysticism, prophesy and visions in the communities, generated a great deal of persecution against them. Marguerite Porete, a French Beguine-mystic, was accused of heresy by the Catholic church and burned at the stake in 1310 in Paris. Her book, The Mirror of Simple Souls, was censured as heresy and, failing to recant its teachings, she was condemned to die.

Unfortunately, their experiences were difficult for society to understand. Thus, they came under heavy religious persecution by the Pope, the bishops and the

Inquisition, until their numbers began to wane by the 17th century.

I hear very few people talk much about the Beguines revival during the 1200s—1600s. Yet, with a focus on intimacy with Jesus Christ, their effect on Belgium, the Netherlands, Northern France and Germany was evident by the wide-spread renewal amongst the middle-class.

For a time, these daring women redefined the role of women in Christian society and developed multiple assemblages with the primary purpose of pursuing Christ. Try as some might to dim the light of the Beguines women, they are even now renowned for their genuine and passionate love for their Savior. Building dynamic, life-changing communities, these women became a refuge to any seeker who yearned to know the Christ of the Beguines women.

Harvest of Potential

God did not create you to live in survival mode. He created you with the intention that you would enjoy your life and thrive—living to your fullest potential in Him. That is what He designed you for and it is His delight. He gets great joy in seeing you walk in the fullness of your potential. He enjoys your enjoyment. He has placed deep wells of potential inside you, which He intends to draw out.

When the Father called you out of your shell to do the greater works (John 14:12) He planned for you to do, He anticipated everything you would need to accomplish His will. It's already inside you waiting to be harvested—to birth your dreams and manifest God's presence.

Just like Adam and Eve were convinced of their failure (Genesis 3:10), we battle the same feelings of inadequacies. Invariably, the lies sown into our roots at the beginning of our lives try desperately to hinder our growth and potential. And just like Adam and Eve, God says to you: "Who told you that you were naked?" (Genesis 3:11 NLT). God sees the lies the enemy has sown in your heart much more clearly than you do, so He calls your attention to it so you can uproot it.

The reality is, there is a war in the heavens over possession of your heart and mind. When you battle with the lies of the enemy, you will begin to see the realization of your potential. It is incredibly vital to heaven and so very necessary to the Earth—you are that important. As you take authority over the lies of the enemy that want to rob you of your confidence, know you are not just wrestling for your own sake, but for the triumph of the kingdom of heaven.

As you stand in confidence to defeat destiny's thief, understand and recognize you stand in the confidence of the entire kingdom of heaven. So, tell that devil he has no chance against you and refuse to give him any place in your life. "Submit yourselves...to God. Resist the devil, and he WILL [literally] FLEE from you" (James 4:7 NIV emphasis mine).

God has placed wells of potential inside of you, and as you draw from it, you bring a great reward to His kingdom. Draw near to Him and He will harvest your potential. Be confident that, "He who began a good work in you will carry it on to completion until the day of Christ Jesus" (Philippians 1:6 NIV).

Psalm 68:11 prophesied the coming of a great army of women who would experience incredible victories for the Kingdom of Christ. God is calling His warrior-women to the frontlines.

Truly, He's prepared you and now He's calling you. He needs you. The harvest is waiting—will you come?

14

Influential Women

"The seventh time around, when the priests sounded the trumpet blast, Joshua commanded the army, 'Shout! For the LORD has given you the city!'" Joshua 6:16 NIV.

WHAT WE AS women have inherited from cultural bias and especially from the church is at best a compromised destiny. From the start, we have had to fight an uphill battle. As women, we've been sent the message in countless ways that we are less. But the truth is, we are not less! We are intelligent! We are capable! We are gifted and wonderfully designed by God! Our goodness is not qualified by how much we serve men or how many babies we give birth to.

God created each of us, male and female, unique and different with different likes and dislikes. Why then do we try to put a rubber stamp on females in an effort to force them into a mold. At best, you will just convince people they are inadequate and are not good enough the way they are, compromising their confidence.

What message have you been sent and what are you sending to the next generation? Is it compromising your destiny, power or purpose in Christ? I've watched the older generation struggle with the burden of a yoke they were not created to carry.

I've heard older women say, "Yes, men are the head, but women are the neck that turns the head!" To the older generation it may seem like an empowering thought, but to the younger generation, it seems like manipulation or an excuse to use your brain. Why not admit men and women are partners in life and, just like the Trinity, we are one and should honor each other as equals (Ephesians 5:25-32).

By honoring women, we teach them to honor themselves and the gifts and abilities God's given them—not apologizing for our intelligence or position of authority. Our uniqueness is important to God. When we stop comparing or being compared, we can appreciate who God's made us to be. Our heavenly Father's opinion about us is the only one that matters.

The Cult of Domesticity

Truly, there is no denying the impact men have had in hindering women's ministries, but the blame cannot be theirs alone. No, in fact, whole movements have been created by women that have impeded women's ministry efforts.

The Victorian era brought great change for women, but not all of the changes were positive. Barbara Welter started a woman's movement now known as the Cult of Domesticity (1800s), which fought against the progress for women's rights made during the Second Great Awakening. In her movement, she argued for the role of a Christian woman to be characterized by extreme traditional views, not strength and character as the Word defines us.

The core belief of her movement was women were to submit to their sphere of home, children and all things domestic. It was thought to be unladylike and ungodly to even want to earn money, or to have a purpose other than the feminine concerns of the home. Although not necessarily negative, nonetheless as they were more rigidly defined by the movement, it essentially created a prison of propriety for women. Anything other than what they deemed as acceptable behavior reduced ones standing as a lady and you and your family could be ostracized by society.

Strengthened by a massive media campaign, this movement strove to define what were the acceptable characteristics of a lady. The primary message conveyed to society was: *women are weak, soft and unintelligent* and, therefore, must submit themselves to the superior care of men. Altogether it reinforced the traditional beliefs that women were second class creations made by a God who designed them that way. Through a sneaky attempt at creating a seemingly noble role for women as useless doll-like creatures, they were, in fact, stripping women of their purpose.

In an attempt to retain power, the message was communicated to women: "*You are weak and unintelligent, so let us run the world for you.*" A true woman was not to participate in public society—that was the man's world. The woman's place was designated to be in the home. A woman was made quite conscious of her supposed inferiority and was indoctrinated by society to believe she needed a man to make her a whole person and therefore submit to him in gratitude due to her weakness.

Through religion, media and education, women were segregated and isolated. Instead of the oneness God had designed, instead of working through life side by side, husband and wife were divided into two spheres of life. Contrary to God's design of mutual respect, men were pitted against women and believed them to be inferior. Rather than a society of mutual humans, we became men and women focused on our differences rather than our likenesses. We were divided—no longer equals.

By society and by family, women were pressured to marry, yet the laws against married women at this time were inconceivable. The minute a woman married, she became a non-person and her personage was swallowed up by that of her husband—she literally did not exist in the eyes of the law. With no other legal means to support herself, a woman was basically forced into marriage whether she wanted to be or not. Which, of course, often led to difficult marriages and abuse.

When a woman entered into marriage, any inheritance or financial resource that belonged to her was instantly forfeited to her husband. She had no legal home and no legal rights to her children. She could not divorce her husband even though he could divorce her. She could not vote, work or defend herself in court. Her identity was completely absorbed into that of her husband.

I believe the life of Barbara Welter stands as a warning to listen to the Lord, the Word and the needs of all women: weakness is not Godly behavior. God created us each with a life's purpose and fulfilling that purpose brings us joy.

Caroline Norton

Caroline Norton was a social reformer and successfully campaigned for married women's rights. Through her efforts the *Custody of Infants Acts* was passed by Parliament in 1839, giving married women legal rights to their own children. She fought to pass the *Matrimonial Causes Act* in 1857, which gave women the legal right to divorce if they had just cause to do so and also, the *Married Women's Property Act* in 1870, which allowed women to own property.

In 1827, Caroline married George Norton, barrister, M.P. He was very jealous and possessive, given to violent, drunken fits of temper. He was emotionally and physically abusive to Caroline. Abuse of a wife by her husband was legal at that time, so she had no recourse to end it.

Caroline did not know her husband well before she married him, and unfortunately found herself trapped in a dangerous marriage. She bore three children, and most of the joy she had in life came from them.

Caroline was incredibly creative and intellectually gifted; she was a writer and composer and brought in money through her writing. However, any money a wife earned at that time went to her husband.

Matters got worse in the family when George lost his position as a member of parliament. He took it out on his family and made life much worse for Caroline. Through a family connection she had with Lord Melbourne, Britain's Prime Minister at the time, she was successful in getting her husband a position as a magistrate (lower-level judge).

Unfortunately, even though she had been

encouraged by her husband to use her connections to advance his career, he became extremely jealous of her relationship with Lord Melbourne. George went so far as to accuse him of having a verbal affair with his wife.

In 1836, George Norton took Lord Melbourne to court, accusing him of having an on-going affair with his wife, Caroline. As ladies were not allowed in court, she was not even able to defend herself against the accusations, for in the eyes of the law, Caroline did not exist. She was legally a non-human. Her identity and personage was absorbed into the legal identity of her husband.

After Lord Melbourne was cleared of the charges and proven innocent, he was treated as a hero in society. Caroline's reputation, however, was destroyed and bore the shame of her husband's accusation regardless of her innocence and was ostracized by society.

Furious over the loss of the court case, George further punished her by taking her children away from her and putting them in the care of his mistress. She was forced out of her own home with no financial means. It was at this time she realized there were no laws to protect her rights and nothing she could do to get her sons back. In the eyes of the law, they were his and she had no right to them. Moreover, she had no legal right to the royalty money she made from her own books; it all went directly to her husband whom she could not legally divorce.

After a time of struggle and starvation, she decided to teach herself the law and found that, though she no longer lived with her husband, she could charge him for her food and lodging. When she did, he refused to pay and the creditors, not recognizing *her* as a legal person, took her husband to court for payment of her bills.

With nothing else to lose, Caroline broke the rules and went to court to defend herself and present her case to the court. Once there, her husband ruthlessly brought up the accusations of a verbal affair with Lord Melbourne, which opened the door for her to tell the court of his extramarital affairs and abuse. Needless to say, she won her case.

She went on to work with politicians to change the laws against women. Parliament passed laws to protect women's interests in marriage and due to her perseverance, married women were now legally recognized by law.

I've often heard complaints about feminists amongst male religious leaders, who've tried to paint the feminist movements as worldly and sinful, but it does not take a difficult study through history to see how terribly untrue that report is. Although some feminist movements have gotten off course at times, most all historical feminists came from very pious backgrounds and strove to help women by simply giving them basic human rights. Some of them are better described as missionaries or patron saints to women of all races, positions and walks of life.

Caroline did not want to lead the life she did, but still she is influential because in her most difficult struggles she persevered and won. She won not just for herself, but for every woman and child who would come after her.

Queen Elizabeth I

Although I'm quite sure you've heard of this next influential woman, I'm not positive you've been made aware of the huge advancement made for women by *Queen Elizabeth I.*

Elizabeth was only three when her mother was put to death by her father because she failed to give him a son. Her father, King Henry the VIII, was the sun, moon and stars to little Elizabeth, yet he had her declared illegitimate and denied royal succession, which, fortunately, he later reversed. While twice narrowly surviving sentences of death, first by her half-brother and then her older half-sister, she lived to succeed her sister, Mary, on the throne in 1558.

Intelligent, as well as clever, twenty-five year old Elizabeth shocked her court by refusing to marry. She had seen the trouble of other queens who'd married and refused to have it thrust upon her. It was believed at that time a queen naturally needed a husband to rule with or for her as co-ruler. It seemed utterly impossible for a woman to rule as her own king, as well as queen, but Elizabeth did.

Her sister, Mary, was a terrible queen and seemed to prove the theory that women were simply unfit to reign. However, Elizabeth was about to completely negate that theory!

While staving off countless attempts to unseat her by her male cousins and then by Pope Pius V in 1570, she ruled as the most successful ruler England ever had. At the beginning of her reign, England was an insignificant country. But by the end, it was a major European power. It is Elizabeth who deserves the credit for laying the foundation for England becoming an extraordinary empire, which reached around the globe.

Having done it all with the guidance of the Lord, Elizabeth had truly developed an intimate relationship with God, always seeking His guidance above all others and placing Him first in her heart. As England was surrounded by Catholic nations who, with the Pope's encouragement, tried to destroy her, she established and protected the newly formed *Protestant* Church of England.

While some historians call her lucky, her life-long relationship with God is an established fact. She unquestionably believed God had, indeed, protected her. Elizabeth trusted God and He surrounded her with wise and honest council. She was also greatly esteemed by her subjects, and for that, she thanked God often in prayer. She followed God and He made her great and as He did, He used her reign to break off a great deal of prejudice against women rulers.

Elizabeth's life as queen was not at all easy or glamorous as you may suppose. Truly, her life was a life of sacrifice and great courage. It was unquestionably difficult for a woman to rule, yet she did. And she was marvelously successful at it. She is an influential woman if only for the example she has set for all of us even now—we have no excuses. If God has called us to it, with His help we will succeed!

Wisdom and strength do not make you less of a woman. No. Indeed, they are qualities anyone should be proud to display. Our lives, whether small or great, influence those around us and you never know who those women may one day become. You may not even realize the encouragement you bring to other women by the way you live. Stand strong! You never know who is watching.

These influential women, of course, are just a couple of the women who have become mentors for thousands who sought the Lord. Indeed, they are an army of women—a mighty throng!

15

Josephine Butler

"And those who are peacemakers will plants seeds of
peace and reap a harvest of righteousness" James 3:18
NLT.

JOSEPHINE BUTLER WAS born the seventh child
of a prominent aristocratic Quaker family in Glendale,
Northumberland UK in 1828. Her family was filled
will strong-minded women. Her father, John Grey,
had been greatly influenced by his mother, Mary, who
was legendary for her hatred of injustice and brought
up her children on stories of the abolitionist
movement, sowing seeds of activism that would
multiply through generations.

John Grey was determined that his daughters be
brought up feeling the impact of his amazing
mother's beliefs and he was extremely proud of
Josephine's accomplishments. When asked about her
unwavering fight against state regulated prostitution
in England, she said of her father, "That they should
ever be indifferent to anything that concerned their
country's good was to him the only marvel."[1]
Brought up in the Moravian Church, Josephine's
mother, Hannah, was very devoted and it was told
that she had received a blessing by John Wesley as a
baby.

Josephine married George Butler, a professor at Oxford University in 1852. Before marrying, George asked her to accept his vision for marriage which was as follows: "Namely, a perfectly equal union, with absolute freedom on both sides for personal initiative in thought and action and for individual development. I am more content to leave you to walk by yourself in the path you shall choose; but I know that I do not leave you alone and unsupported, for His arm will guide, strengthen and protect you."[2]

Josephine and George had four children, three boys and then a daughter. Josephine was thirty-five when her little Eva fell down the stairs and died at the age of five. Desperately brokenhearted, Josephine sought the Lord for a cause to fight for to ease the pain she felt in the death of her beloved daughter. Thankfully, the Father answered her prayer.

Contagious Diseases Act

Giving her the very special calling of fighting for women against the regulated injustice of prostitution in England, she admirably fought her cause while her reputation and life were in constant jeopardy. The "surgical rape" of women, as Josephine called it, is an outrage that is almost forgotten. In Victorian England, the police force was granted powers to force any woman they *suspected* of being a prostitute to undergo mandatory medical examinations for sexually transmitted diseases, some as young as twelve years old. Women who refused to submit willingly would be arrested and incarcerated.

As a means of stopping the spread of venereal disease, Queen Victoria signed into law the

Contagious Diseases Act in 1869 that regulated state prostitution. The law had already been implemented in much of Europe, and many governments, in an attempt to hinder the spread of disease through prostitution, regulated it. Women were forcibly registered by police as prostitutes and were regularly (usually weekly) tested for diseases. If they were found to be infected, they were thrown into lock hospitals, which specialized in treating venereal diseases and were largely connected to the military, until they recovered.

Women were not allowed to work, except for in service as a maid or through prostitution. Due to their earning limitations, women were very vulnerable if they did not have male protection and help. Prostitution was a last resort for all these women, many of them got into prostitution against their will and once known as a prostitute many women committed suicide due to the shame of it.

Although men who frequented prostitutes were never tested for disease, any woman who was unaccompanied at night could be snatched off the street and processed as a prostitute by even the suspicions of the police. If she protested, she was thrown into prison until she confessed to being a prostitute and would sign a so-called voluntary waver for regular testing.

For the daughters of the poor, this was terrifying. If a young girl was suspected of prostitution she would lose her position of employment as a servant and her registration as a prostitute would inhibit her from marrying. Some of the young girls could not even read the forms they signed confessing their occupation as prostitutes. The age of consent in

Britain was twelve, so many of the victims of this law were very young.

This law regulating prostitution gave the police totalitarian power over women of poor families who had little or no protection from them. They could order mandatory genital testing for all prostitutes at any time. Once registered, these women literally lost their humanity and became inhuman: mere numbered, inspected and ticketed human flesh—all from the families of the poor. If you were a woman of poor rank, you could be labeled and registered as a prostitute simply at the whim of the authorities in order to fulfill the pampered desires of rich men.

Since they were thought to be the lowest form of humans in society, they were regularly abused, physically, sexually and emotionally, while being examined. The tests were so horrible, many women became sterile afterward. Any woman had only to be accused of being a prostitute to be rushed off for examination or, as Josephine called it: surgically raped. They endured these horrendous examinations, not for their own good, but so their bodies could be used by men. The prisons they were sent to if found to be infected were, as Josephine put it, *hellish* and, tragically, many of the women died.

Josephine Butler entered this barbaric inferno to minister to the prostitutes. What would have been unthinkable to other women of her rank, she felt passionately as her calling. As an angel of mercy, she entered the lives of the prostitutes and treated them as equals. Calling them sisters, she treated them as if they were her own daughters.

Wanting to restore an essence of their humanity, Josephine cared for some of the women in her own home with the help of her husband and three sons. For some of these women, it was the first time they had ever experienced human kindness and the effect on their lives was transforming. Unfortunately, many of the young women she brought into her home were beyond her help and died from the diseases they had contracted from the men. Still, Josephine filled every possible room of her house with rescued young women from the strangle-hold of poverty and prostitution.

Overwhelmed by their need, she and her political proponents decided the law regulating prostitution had to be repealed. Although Josephine was a small woman in poor health, she fought for these women with unwavering dedication as though she were fighting for her own little daughter.

Ladies National Association

Josephine created the Ladies National Association for the Repeal of the Contagious Diseases Act. With the help of her religious, as well as political connections, she campaigned vehemently. Despite the defamation of her character, physical attacks and even attempts against her life, she was simply relentless.

In her speeches, she often quoted the abolitionist, William Lloyd Garrison, saying, "I will be harsh as truth, and as uncompromising as justice. I am in earnest—I will not equivocate—and I will be heard."[3] And also Quaker minister, the abolitionist John Woolman, who said, "Only love enough, and all things are possible to you."[4]

What Josephine continually encountered was a society which had so hated the sin of prostitution, they lost sight of the humanity of its victims—young girls. She spent a great deal of her time trying to restore their humanity in an effort to enrage the public against their plight. To a conference of men she spoke of the young girls who turned to prostitution to keep from starving to death, "Two pence, gentlemen, is the price in England of a poor girl's honour."[5]

Many men became enraged at the thought of losing the legalization of prostitution and hired gangs to intimidate or hurt her. They publicly posted daily descriptions of what she was wearing so the mobs could harass her. Joining her meetings, they would harangue her to try to silence her.

After one of her meetings, Josephine was shut up in a random store room to keep her hidden from the mob and a young prostitute found her there. In the store room, the young woman sat in awe of Josephine who risked her life to fight for her and other prostitutes like her. Whispering to Josephine, she said, "Are you the lady the mob are after? Oh, what a shame to treat a lady so," which encouraged Josephine very much. After another meeting, Josephine was rescued by a local grocer who promised to protect her with his life.

While speaking in a barn to a group of women, the mob surrounded the barn, locked them in and set it on fire. They only escaped as one woman threw herself at the men so the rest of the women could escape through a latched door in the floor.

Despite the ferocious attacks against her, she prevailed and generated great outrage in England as she further investigated the crimes of flesh-peddlers. It was found that girls as young as three were being purchased from Britain and sent to the European continent and sold as sex-slaves to well-known aristocratic men all over Europe. Literally, by the dozens, little girls were sent to feed the voraciously perverse appetites of the rich.

Persecution and Harassment

Police harassment and persecution of poor women was notorious. One such story of a woman named Mrs. Percy gained national attention. Mrs. Percy had recently been widowed and, solely because she was impoverished, was watched by the police. Convinced she would turn to prostitution, they harassed her, trying to force her to register as a prostitute. Warning landlords of her *bad character*, they slandered her. Overwhelmed by their constant harassment, Mrs. Percy killed herself instead of facing the disgrace of being labeled a prostitute. After her death, they went after her young daughter, but she was rescued, thank heaven, by Josephine.

In a speech shortly after the incident, Josephine spoke for *all women*, "We rebel! I grant that this is not the language of science; it is not the formula of statistics or of hygienic deduction; no it is simply the outburst of that condemnation which has been kept voiceless through centuries... it is the protest of all womanhood, a cry of horror, an appeal to justice."[6]

In a speech given in Albert Hall, Josephine exposed the grievous wrongs imposed on the poor by the rich. She demanded of her political opponents, "If prostitution is a necessity, I call upon Mr. Cave, Colonel Alexander, and Mr. Gathorne Hardy each to contribute a daughter."[7]

Josephine suffered greatly from the perverse revelations she found in her investigations and would often have to travel south to regain her health. But, miraculously, after sixteen long years, Queen Victoria and her government repealed the act in 1886.

Josephine's Influence Reaches India

After the repeal of the act, a report reached Josephine that the British military in India had complaints of the *quality* of prostitutes they were being *provided.* Thus, the military asked for "sufficiently attractive" women to be *found and purchased by the government* for their use.

Although her health was declining, Josephine wasted no time in responding. God provided two American missionary women who traveled to India to investigate the situation and see if the repeal of the Contagious Diseases Act was enforced. What they found simply appalled the people.

The women visited ten military barracks and found prostitutes in all of them. They found hundreds of Indian women, most of them very young, housed in large buildings for the use of the troops. The majority of the girls were widows, married very young (ages 10-12) and sold to the army by their husband's families. The women were terrified of the violent, drunken rages of the soldiers, and all of them were still subjected to the examinations of the Contagious Diseases Act.

Even through her widowhood, Josephine continued to fight similar battles in Geneva and Italy and fought unwaveringly for truth until she went home to the Lord in 1906 at the age of 79.

George Butler

Although Josephine was the main force of their abolitionist movement against sex-slavery, she and George worked together as he held an integral role in their work. George was a very forward thinking and Christlike man. He not only blessed her work, but worked with her, as well as supporting it publicly and privately as he was needed.

He believed strongly in her equality and voiced praise for her incredibly gifted political mind. If any men called on him for political advice, he would stop and tell them before answering that he would first have to consult with his wife to seek her council for them.

Josephine and George Butler were not just *egalitarian* in their thinking in relating to each other as man and wife, their marriage and their lives were based on the Word of God—they were a team! "What God has joined together, let no man separate!" (Mark 10:9 NIV).

Together, the Butlers were a feminist-team, *because* they were genuine Christians, passionate about portraying the kind Christianity they saw exemplified in the Word of God. Though it often put them at odds with the traditional views of some in the church, they continued on with the work of Christ.

Josephine's activist methods became a model for early suffragist movements. She believed strongly that *women would not be safe from degradation until the value of all women was established*. Surely, I agree, men will always be in danger of degradation and abuse toward women until they are taught to honor and respect them as equals.

I have been influenced more by Josephine Butler than any other historical account of Christian activism. She is a wonderful example to all of us. If we could remember her determination, strength and selfless love, we would not doubt our own capabilities as women.

16

Hold On To Your Crown

"Since you have kept my command to endure patiently, I
will also keep you from the hour of trial that is going to
come on the whole world to test the inhabitants of the
earth. I am coming soon. Hold on to what you have, so
that no one will take your crown" Revelation 3:10-11 NIV.

AFTER MY DAUGHTER, Cassandra, suffered so
much at the Christian school where she'd first
encountered the bias against women, we talked to the
principal who was very upset by what the teacher had
done. Showing signs of remorse, he was visibly
touched when he heard how Cassandra was affected
by this teaching. Up to that point, the church attached
to the school taught this teaching annually, but after
that interview, they chose no longer to teach it. He
promised then he would take care to see this didn't
happen again and he meant it.

In spite of the principal's assurance things would
change, we did not feel comfortable leaving her in the
school and put our children in another Christian
school. However, that school only went through
eighth grade. After she finished there, we were unsure
of what to do and decided to put her in a public high
school.

After a year, we decided we could not leave her in

public school and sought the Lord for His direction for our daughter. I was not in favor of sending her back to the Christian school that had caused her so much pain, but it was the only Christian school in the area that offered high school classes. As we prayed for direction, the Lord promised if we put her back in the Christian high school, He would bless her.

Although the Lord had promised to bless Cassandra, it was still not easy for her. Indeed, it was very difficult. Both the school and church, which was attached to the school, stopped teaching the gender bias they had previously taught against women. However, the young boys attending the school had already received the message they were superior to females and let them know it.

Watching her endure the struggles she experienced, sometimes it was all I could do to keep from pulling her back out. I clung to the promise the Lord had given me for her life, that He would bless her there. Still, the onslaught against her was horrendous and continuous, not just from the school kids, but, it seemed, from every aspect of her life. I simply couldn't believe the attack against her. I started to reason to myself, "Why is this happening to her?"

There was a great deal of persecution from every direction, but especially from the boys who thought it was their mission to straighten her out. One such boy came to our home and literally harassed her with his version of the truth based on one scripture he had only *heard*, yet never read for himself and a truck-load of irrational ideas about women. I reasoned *passionately* with the young man, and while I was there he stopped. But he would follow her from room to room to continue his onslaught. His goal wasn't to reasonably debate a doctrinal teaching in an effort to learn, but to bombard her with cruelty. He was motivated by hatred.

Cassandra was truly being harassed, and though I had never kicked any teenager out of our home before, I did that one! I threw every last teen out the door that day and told my son to never invite him back. He agreed wholeheartedly. Because there was nothing redemptive that could come from that relationship, it was just an entrance for the enemy to destroy.

When she was eighteen, she dated one young man from the school. Although he was a nice boy, he had also adopted the traditional view of women. He wanted to marry her, but he did not want a wife in ministry. He didn't even want a wife who sang at church, which she was doing at the time. Moreover, he thought the idea of my ministry was literally revolting.

Defending Her Crown

In Cassandra's relationship struggles, I saw a pattern begin to emerge in her life. Although the calling she'd received as a child was always tucked away in the back of her mind, she had lost her passion and zeal to reach the lost. Yet, the more the enemy tried to talk her out of her calling through boys, friends or other circumstances, the more she fought to defend it and the stronger it took hold of her. Suddenly, I was seeing in her the similar passion she had as a child, the tenacity to stubbornly stand for the Lord and to fight for others.

Besides the harassment for her beliefs, she was

also bullied by some of the so-called popular girls at the Christian school who were insecure and fought hard against anyone they felt was a threat. Cassandra was and is a very beautiful girl and of course they felt threatened by her. She endured a great deal of slander from them, not only about her, but our family as well. Yet, we also saw how the Lord continually protected her in this. Because of the Godly life she lived, no one believed the negative talk about her. And in her defense, the hearers became angry at the girls who had started the rumors against her.

As she grew stronger and stronger, tougher and tougher, she became more and more vocal to fight for herself and other kids. Anyone who was not accepted or lonely, anyone in anyway needing a friend, clung to Cassandra for strength, strength of character she had because she endured the persecution and let it mold her into a fighter.

She hadn't really realized it, but by her senior year in high school, she had amassed a following of young people who looked to her for strength and guidance. She stuck up for them against the persecution of the bullies. And when it came time for the whole high school to vote for their choice for the school's homecoming queen that year, she was their overwhelming choice.

I remembered standing and watching all the girls from her class who had made high school so difficult for her, and now the popular girls confidently believed they would be crowned queen. Yet, it was not they, but Cassandra, the girl they had rejected and slandered, who walked away with the crown that day. I looked around at the auditorium and saw a crowd of people united in applauding my daughter for who she was and not who she wasn't, as the announcer proclaimed loudly over the microphone, "This year's homecoming queen is.....Cassandra Boyson!"

Cassandra's heavenly Father placed a crown on her head and confidence in her heart. And just as He promised, He had blessed her. He had prepared "a feast for [her] in the presence of [her] enemies. [He] honored [her] by anointing [her] head with oil" (Psalm 23:5 NLT). Out of something ugly, the Father had created something quite beautiful and our cup was overflowing!

It had been a difficult journey, but what a reward. Of course, the crown was not the reward she received for her perseverance, but the outward sign of the inward work God had performed in and through her. Restoring her heart and her calling, her testimony ministers to women all over the world. Grown women come to me in tears as they feel the healing power of the Holy Spirit ministering to them through her testimony!

I thought that day when Cassandra received her crown of the scripture in Revelation 3:10-12, "*Since you have kept my command to endure patiently, I will also keep you from the hour of trial that is going to come on the whole world to test the inhabitants of the earth. I am coming soon. Hold on to what you have, so that no one will take your crown.*

The one who is victorious I will make a pillar in the temple of my God. Never again will they leave it. I will write on them the name of my God and the name of the city of my God, the new Jerusalem, which is coming down out of heaven from my God; and I will also write on them my new name" (NIV).

As Her Mother

I tried so hard to protect Cassandra from the trials and persecutions the enemy launched at her, but in the end, it was the trials that made her who God wanted her to become. I thought it was weakening her, but God knew it was making her an iron tower for others to run to for protection. She was a gift God was building for the nations and her testimony is what God built in me as well.

As I fought to deliver Cassandra from the grip of the lies thrown at her, I had no idea how God would use it. I had no idea then how her pain and my desperation as her mother would change the hearts and minds of women everywhere, building an army of women by delivering them from any hesitation to grab hold of their callings. And they, in turn, will change the world!

Our struggles together equipped us for the battles that lay before us and "when troubles come your way, consider it an opportunity for great joy. For you know that when your faith is tested, your endurance has a chance to grow. So let it grow, for when your endurance is fully developed, you will be perfect and complete, needing nothing" (James 1:2-4 NLT).

In Conclusion

For His Daughters

AS A WOMAN who are you really? Who do you think you are and why do you think God created you? Were you created to be just an accent to society, surrounded by other more important people who seem to matter more than you? Or were you, yes YOU, created for a divine purpose, and if so, what do you think that purpose is?

Your heavenly Father created you as a woman *on purpose;* your gender was never an accident—it was His design. He made you female on purpose, because you were what He wanted—you are His delight. He has great plans and hopes for everyday of your life, and He enjoys watching you fulfill and walk in everything He, as your loving Father, has set in place for your life.

He loves you so much that He made you in His image. "God created human beings in his own image. In the image of God he created them; male and female he created them" Genesis 1:27 NLT. Yes, you were made in God's image—a work of art, *His magnum opus.* Both men and women are made in God's image, yet do they know it? Do women really realize they were made in God's image as much as the male gender?

Truly, you are made in God's image and if others have declared you as a woman to be second-class because of gender bias, then truly they are calling God second-class. For indeed, He made you; He fashioned and designed you in His image and He very much loves what He made in you!

Even if your earthly father and mother desert you, He will hold you close (Psalm 27:10). Truly, if no other human person ever sees your true value, your heavenly Father does. He has always seen your worth, and longs for others to see it as well. Through Him, the world will see the value of your life!

Your Father has seen your struggles and the pain you have endured. And by His Spirit, He will deliver you from the lies of the enemy. He will strengthen you and build you into a mighty tower of His power! He wants you to know exactly who you were created to be and how much He dearly, dearly loves you.

You are His masterpiece, the grand finale of His design. You are His Magnum Opus!

Victoria has created a study guide
for this material:

God's Magnum Opus
Challenge for Women

Other Books by Victoria Boyson

The Birth of Your Destiny: Just like a baby hidden in the womb, so are the promises God has given to us. He speaks to us of our future as if to conceive within us His will and purpose for our lives. Experience an impartation of God's grace and faith to fulfill all that God has for you through this powerful and insightful book.

His Passionate Pursuit: Victoria challenges you to embrace the captivating revelations of His passion for you - His beloved bride. It is an invitation to an awakening encounter with God. His Passionate Pursuit is a portal to heaven, unleashing God's presence into your life, empowering you with an impartation from His heart.

Awakening: The Deep Sleep (A Visionary Journey): With the fate of the world in the balance, Beloved must rise above the deceptive snares of her adversaries to fulfill her calling: to pursue the prophetic host and liberate the slumbering army of the Lord. Destined to wage war against the darkness, the army must be awakened to destroy the enemy's grasp on this world.

To contact the author or to order more copies of God's Magnum Opus, please visit her website at www.VictoriaBoyson.com.

God's Magnum Opus is also available through Amazon.com, Christian bookstores and other online bookstores. It is also available as an eBook, purchasable through Amazon.com.

Follow Victoria Boyson on Facebook, Twitter and Goodreads.

Check out the many resources on her website and sign up for her enewsletter at: www.VictortiaBoyson.com.

90264141R00106

Made in the USA
Middletown, DE
22 September 2018